Better Homes and Gardens®

fresh and simple™

20-minute super suppers

Better Homes and Gardens® Books
Des Moines, Iowa

All of us at Better Homes and Gardens® Books
are dedicated to providing you with the information and ideas you need to create delicious foods. We welcome your comments and suggestions. Write to us at Better Homes and Gardens® Books, Cookbook Editorial Department, RW-240, 1716 Locust St., Des Moines, IA 50309-3023.

If you would like to order additional copies of any of our books, please check with your local bookstore.

Our seal assures you that every recipe in *20-Minute Super Suppers* has been tested in the Better Homes and Gardens® Test Kitchen. This means that each recipe is practical and reliable and meets our high standards for taste appeal. We guarantee your satisfaction with this book for as long as you own it.

Pictured on front cover: Tuscan Lamb Chop Skillet (see recipe, *page 23*)

Pictured on page 1: Cumin Chicken with Nectarine Salsa (see recipe, *page 16*)

Better Homes and Gardens® Books
An imprint of Meredith® Books

Fresh and Simple™ *20-Minute Super Suppers*
Editor: Lisa Holderness
Contributing Editors: Karen A. Levin, Spectrum Communication Services
Contributing Writer: Lisa Kingsley
Designer: Craig Hanken
Copy Editor: Jennifer Speer Ramundt
Electronic Production Coordinator: Paula Forest
Editorial and Design Assistants: Judy Bailey, Jennifer Norris, Karen Schirm
Test Kitchen Director: Sharon Stilwell
Test Kitchen Product Supervisor: Jill Hoefler
Food Stylists: Susan Brown Draudt, Janet Pittman
Photographer: Jim Krantz, Kritsada Panichgul
Prop Stylist: Nancy Wall Hopkins
Production Director: Douglas M. Johnston
Production Manager: Pam Kvitne
Assistant Prepress Manager: Marjorie J. Schenkelberg

Meredith® Books
Editor in Chief: James D. Blume
Design Director: Matt Strelecki
Managing Editor: Gregory H. Kayko

Director, Sales & Marketing, Retail: Michael A. Peterson
Director, Sales & Marketing, Special Markets: Rita McMullen
Director, Sales & Marketing, Home & Garden Center Channel: Ray Wolf
Director, Operations: Valerie Wiese

Vice President, General Manager: Jamie L. Martin

Better Homes and Gardens® Magazine
Editor in Chief: Jean LemMon
Executive Food Editor: Nancy Byal

Meredith Publishing Group
President, Publishing Group: Christopher M. Little
Vice President, Consumer Marketing and Development: Hal Oringer

Meredith Corporation
Chairman and Chief Executive Officer: William T. Kerr

Chairman of the Executive Committee: E. T. Meredith III

contents

put the fresh
back in dinnertime

Fresh and healthful... **Different but doable...** Food with personality...

Tall order for a weeknight dinner? Sure, but that's what busy cooks told

Better Homes and Gardens® Books they craved. And that's what you'll get

with every recipe in our new *Fresh and Simple*™ series. After all, if your

busy family drops everything to gather for mealtime, don't you deserve

more than memorable conversation? The key to *20-Minute Super*

Suppers, and all of the books in this series, is the use of fresh,

innovative flavors created from easy-to-find produce and seasonings.

The prep time for every recipe is minimal and so is the mess, leaving

you with a luscious meal and plenty of time to savor every bite.

chicken
features

keys-style citrus chicken

The tropical-island-inspired cooking of the Florida Keys draws on the best of both of its worlds. Here, it combines fresh Florida citrus with the Caribbean penchant for fiery peppers. Soak up the delicious juice with hot cooked rice.

Start to finish: 20 minutes   Makes 4 servings

Rinse chicken; pat dry. In a large skillet cook chicken and garlic in butter over medium heat for 8 to 10 minutes or until chicken is tender and no longer pink, turning chicken once and stirring garlic occasionally.

Meanwhile, in a small bowl combine lime peel, lime juice, ginger, and red pepper; set aside. Peel orange. Reserving juice, cut orange in half lengthwise, then cut crosswise into slices. Add any reserved orange juice and the lime juice mixture to skillet. Place orange slices on top of chicken. Cook, covered, for 1 to 2 minutes or until heated through. Spoon any reserved drippings over chicken to serve.

Nutrition facts per serving: 167 cal., 6 g total fat (3 g sat. fat), 67 mg chol., 84 mg sodium, 5 g carbo., 1 g fiber, 22 g pro. Daily values: 4% vit. A, 34% vit. C, 2% calcium, 5% iron

4 large skinless, boneless chicken breast halves (about 1 pound total)

2 or 3 cloves garlic, peeled and thinly sliced

1 tablespoon butter or margarine

1 teaspoon finely shredded lime peel

2 tablespoons lime juice

¼ teaspoon ground ginger

⅛ teaspoon crushed red pepper

1 orange

the great tastes of garlic

Garlic can be roasted, braised, baked or, as it is in this recipe, sautéed. Cooking of any kind caramelizes the sugars in garlic, mellowing its pungent smell and taming its assertive flavor. Because it is sautéed with the chicken in Keys-Style Citrus Chicken, the garlic cooks long enough to turn light brown. This adds a toasty flavor that pairs well with the tangy lime juice.

spring vegetable stew

Spring has sprung—and so has supper. Pick the tiniest and tenderest leeks, asparagus, new potatoes, baby carrots, squash, or green beans to brighten this creamy potage.

8

2½ cups prepared fresh spring
    vegetables*

1 teaspoon olive oil or cooking oil

1 cup reduced-sodium chicken broth

½ cup refrigerated light alfredo sauce

1 teaspoon snipped fresh tarragon
    or thyme

1 cup cubed smoked or roasted
    chicken (5 ounces)

¼ cup finely shredded smoked
    Jarlsberg or Parmesan cheese
    (1 ounce)

Start to finish: 20 minutes   Makes 3 servings

In a large saucepan cook and stir vegetables in hot oil over medium-high heat for 3 minutes. Stir in broth, alfredo sauce, and herb. Bring to boiling; reduce heat. Simmer, covered, about 5 minutes or until the vegetables are tender. Stir in chicken; cook and stir until heated through. Sprinkle each serving with cheese.

Nutrition facts per serving: 324 cal., 18 g total fat (8 g sat. fat), 63 mg chol., 962 mg sodium, 25 g carbo., 3 g fiber, 17 g pro. Daily values: 63% vit. A, 20% vit. C, 18% calcium, 12% iron

Note: Choose from sliced leeks, asparagus pieces, cubed new potatoes, halved baby carrots, sliced zucchini or yellow summer squash, or cut green beans.

the art of picking your veggies

When choosing a mix of vegetables for Spring Vegetable Stew, pick your favorites, keeping an eye out for a balance of color and texture (bright green asparagus with vivid orange carrots, for instance, or creamy new potatoes with crisp-tender green beans). For added convenience, look for precut vegetables at your market's salad bar or a stir-fry mix in the produce department.

fettuccine verona

Named for the city of Romeo and Juliet, this romantic red-pepper pasta studded with dried tomatoes goes together so fast, you'll have time to linger over the result (and perhaps even sip a glass of wine).

Start to finish: 18 minutes   Makes 4 servings

Using kitchen scissors, cut fettuccine strands in half. Cook pasta in lightly salted water according to package directions; drain. Return pasta to hot pan.

Meanwhile, rinse chicken; pat dry. Drain the ¼ cup tomatoes, reserving 2 tablespoons of the oil from jar. Set reserved tomatoes aside. In a large skillet heat 1 tablespoon of the reserved oil over medium-high heat. Add zucchini; cook and stir for 2 to 3 minutes or until crisp-tender. Remove from skillet. Add remaining 1 tablespoon oil to skillet. Add chicken; cook and stir for 2 to 3 minutes or until no longer pink.

Add chicken, zucchini, and reserved tomatoes to cooked pasta; toss gently to combine. Sprinkle each serving with cheese. Season with pepper to taste.

Nutrition facts per serving: 381 cal., 14 g total fat (1 g sat. fat), 40 mg chol., 334 mg sodium, 40 g carbo., 3 g fiber, 24 g pro. Daily values: 8% vit. A, 16% vit. C, 13% calcium, 13% iron

1 **9-ounce package refrigerated red sweet pepper fettuccine**

8 **ounces skinless, boneless chicken breast strips for stir-frying**

¼ **of a 7-ounce jar oil-packed dried tomato strips or pieces (¼ cup)**

1 **large zucchini or yellow summer squash, halved lengthwise and sliced (about 2 cups)**

½ **cup finely shredded Parmesan, Romano, or Asiago cheese (2 ounces)**

thai chicken wraps

Join the wrap rage with this all-in-one meal of Pacific Rim flavors: sautéed chicken, a confetti of gingered vegetables, and a sweet and savory peanut sauce.

Start to finish: 20 minutes   Makes 6 servings

Wrap tortillas in paper towels. Microwave on 100% power (high) for 30 seconds to soften. (Or, wrap tortillas in foil. Heat in a 350° oven for 10 minutes.)

Meanwhile, rinse chicken; pat dry. In a small bowl combine garlic salt and pepper. Add chicken; toss to coat evenly. In a large skillet cook and stir seasoned chicken in hot oil over medium-high heat for 2 to 3 minutes or until no longer pink. Remove from skillet; keep warm. Add broccoli, onion, and gingerroot to skillet. Cook and stir for 2 to 3 minutes or until vegetables are crisp-tender.

To assemble, spread each tortilla with about 1 tablespoon peanut sauce. Top with chicken strips and vegetable mixture. Roll up each tortilla, securing with a toothpick. Serve immediately with remaining sauce.

Peanut Sauce: In a small saucepan combine ¼ cup sugar, ¼ cup creamy peanut butter, 3 tablespoons soy sauce, 3 tablespoons water, 2 table-spoons cooking oil, and 1 teaspoon bottled minced garlic. Heat until sugar is dissolved, stirring frequently. Makes about ⅔ cup.

Nutrition facts per serving: 330 cal., 16 g total fat (3 g sat. fat), 30 mg chol., 911 mg sodium, 30 g carbo., 3 g fiber, 17 g pro. Daily values: 3% vit. A, 39% vit. C, 4% calcium, 11% iron

- 6 8- to 10-inch plain, red, and/or green flour tortillas
- 12 ounces skinless, boneless chicken breast strips for stir-frying
- ½ teaspoon garlic salt
- ¼ to ½ teaspoon pepper
- 1 tablespoon cooking oil
- 4 cups packaged shredded broccoli (broccoli slaw mix)
- 1 medium red onion, cut into thin wedges
- 1 teaspoon grated gingerroot
- 1 recipe Peanut Sauce

chicken with poached pears & fennel

No need to arduously plan for this perfectly autumnal meal. A fall fruit and anise-flavored fennel add seasonal flavor to this dish. Try serving it with hot, buttered egg noodles.

12

1 **fennel bulb (about 1 pound)**

12 **ounces skinless, boneless chicken breast strips for stir-frying**

1 **tablespoon cooking oil**

1 **cup apple juice**

1 **teaspoon five-spice powder**

¼ **teaspoon salt**

2 **medium pears**

1 **tablespoon cornstarch**

2 **tablespoons white wine vinegar**

Start to finish: 20 minutes   Makes 4 servings

Cut off and discard upper stalks of fennel, reserving a few leafy tops for garnish; set aside. Remove any wilted outer layers; cut off a thin slice from base. Wash fennel and cut into thin slices (you should have about 1¼ cups). Rinse chicken; pat dry.

In a large skillet cook and stir chicken in hot oil over medium-high heat for 2 to 3 minutes or until no longer pink. Carefully stir in the sliced fennel, ¾ cup of the apple juice, the five-spice powder, and salt. Bring to boiling; reduce heat. Simmer, covered, for 4 to 5 minutes or until fennel is crisp-tender, stirring occasionally. Meanwhile, core and slice pears; set aside.

Combine remaining ¼ cup apple juice and cornstarch; add to chicken mixture in skillet. Cook and stir until thickened and bubbly. Add vinegar; cook and stir 1 minute more. Add pear slices; cook and stir gently until pears are heated through. Garnish with reserved fennel tops.

Nutrition facts per serving: 217 cal., 6 g total fat (1 g sat. fat), 45 mg chol., 190 mg sodium, 25 g carbo., 10 g fiber, 17 g pro. Daily values: 0% vit. A, 12% vit. C, 3% calcium, 8% iron

warm couscous salad

In Morocco, where couscous is king, the tiny pasta is made into elaborate dishes with meat, vegetables, seafood, and complex mixtures of spices. This version is fresh, full-flavored, and decidedly easier!

Start to finish: 20 minutes   Makes 4 servings

Rinse chicken; pat dry. Cut into 1-inch pieces. In a large saucepan cook and stir chicken in hot oil over medium-high heat for 3 to 4 minutes or until no longer pink. Add broth; bring to boiling. Stir in couscous. Cover; remove from heat. Let stand about 5 minutes or until liquid is absorbed.

Stir cucumber, tomatoes, green onion, mint, and salad dressing into couscous mixture. Serve warm.

Nutrition facts per serving: 335 cal., 9 g total fat (2 g sat. fat), 41 mg chol., 491 mg sodium, 43 g carbo., 8 g fiber, 20 g pro. Daily values: 7% vit. A, 27% vit. C, 2% calcium, 15% iron

dinner's in the bag with bottled dressing

Although homemade dressing is the ideal, bottled dressing comes in handy when time is short—and there are some good ones on the market. The recipe for this chicken-and-grains salad calls for fat-free or reduced-calorie Caesar dressing to keep the fat grams in check. If you prefer the taste of regular instead of fat-free dressing, by all means use it. For a lighter-tasting dressing, drizzle this salad with a vinaigrette.

12 ounces skinless, boneless chicken thighs

1 tablespoon cooking oil

1 14½-ounce can reduced-sodium chicken broth

1 cup quick-cooking couscous

1 small cucumber, halved lengthwise and sliced

2 tomatoes, chopped (1 cup)

¼ cup sliced green onion

¼ cup snipped fresh mint

¼ cup bottled fat-free or reduced-calorie Caesar salad dressing

mexican chicken posole

In parts of Mexico, one day a week is designated as "posole day." Shops and businesses close early and people retire to temporary posole "restaurants" to enjoy a steaming bowl of this hearty soup. See what all the fuss is about (without all the fuss).

12 ounces skinless, boneless chicken thighs or breast halves

3 to 4 teaspoons Mexican seasoning or chili powder

2 teaspoons cooking oil or olive oil

1 red or yellow sweet pepper, cut into bite-size pieces (¾ cup)

2 14½-ounce cans reduced-sodium or regular chicken broth

1 15-ounce can hominy or black-eyed peas, rinsed and drained

Salsa, light dairy sour cream, and/or lime wedges (optional)

Start to finish: 18 minutes   Makes 4 servings

Rinse chicken; pat dry. Cut into 1-inch pieces. Sprinkle chicken with Mexican seasoning; toss to coat evenly. In a large saucepan cook and stir seasoned chicken in hot oil over medium-high heat for 3 minutes. Add sweet pepper; cook and stir about 1 minute more or until chicken is no longer pink.

Carefully add broth and hominy. Bring to boiling; reduce heat. Simmer, covered, about 3 minutes or until heated through. If desired, serve with salsa, sour cream, and/or lime wedges.

Nutrition facts per serving: 192 cal., 8 g total fat (2 g sat. fat), 41 mg chol., 905 mg sodium, 14 g carbo., 1 g fiber, 15 g pro. Daily values: 21% vit. A, 52% vit. C, 2% calcium, 10% iron

cumin chicken
with nectarine salsa

A slightly sweet fresh fruit salsa is the perfect foil for smoky grilled chicken enhanced with the aromatic and earthy flavor of cumin. Serve it with warm tortillas, black beans, and a squeeze of lime. (Pictured on page 1.)

4 large skinless, boneless chicken breast halves (about 1 pound total)

1 tablespoon lime juice

1 to 1½ teaspoons ground cumin

½ cup chunky salsa

⅓ cup chopped nectarine or refrigerated mango slices

2 tablespoons snipped fresh cilantro

Lime wedges (optional)

Start to finish: 20 minutes   Makes 4 servings

Preheat gas grill* or broiler. Rinse chicken; pat dry. Brush chicken with lime juice; sprinkle evenly with cumin. Grill chicken on the rack of an uncovered grill directly over medium heat or broil for 12 to 15 minutes or until chicken is tender and no longer pink, turning once.

Meanwhile, for nectarine salsa, in a small bowl stir together salsa, nectarine, and cilantro. Spoon over chicken. If desired, serve with lime.

Nutrition facts per serving: 144 cal., 4 g total fat (1 g sat. fat), 59 mg chol., 167 mg sodium, 5 g carbo., 0 g fiber, 22 g pro. Daily values: 6% vit. A, 18% vit. C, 2% calcium, 11% iron

Note: Charcoal grill may be used, but allow extra time for coals to reach proper temperature.

side of beans on the double

Give canned black beans a kick with a few extra seasonings, then heat through and serve in just minutes. Rinse and drain one 15-ounce can black beans and place in a medium saucepan. Add half of a 4½-ounce can diced green chili peppers, drained; 1½ teaspoons ground chili powder; and ½ teaspoon ground oregano. Heat through. Stir in 1 tablespoon snipped fresh cilantro. Season to taste with salt and pepper.

chicken & asparagus sauté

A touch of butter, white wine, and *herbes de Provence*—a savory herb blend including thyme, rosemary, marjoram, and often lavender (which grows in profusion on the hillsides of Provence)—gives this dish a French accent.

Start to finish: 20 minutes   Makes 4 servings

Snap off and discard woody bases from asparagus. Bias-slice asparagus into 1-inch pieces (you should have about 1½ cups); set aside.

Rinse chicken; pat dry. In a shallow dish combine flour and herbes de Provence. Coat chicken with flour mixture. In a large nonstick skillet cook seasoned chicken in butter over medium-high heat for 3 minutes. Turn chicken; add asparagus, carrots, and wine. Simmer, uncovered, about 8 minutes more or until chicken is tender and no longer pink and vegetables are crisp-tender, stirring vegetables occasionally.

Nutrition facts per serving: 192 cal., 5 g total fat (2 g sat. fat), 65 mg chol., 87 mg sodium, 7 g carbo., 2 g fiber, 24 g pro. Daily values: 84% vit. A, 31% vit. C, 3% calcium, 10% iron

- **12 ounces asparagus spears**
- **4 large skinless, boneless chicken breast halves (about 1 pound total)**
- **1 tablespoon all-purpose flour**
- **2 teaspoons herbes de Provence or Cajun seasoning**
- **2 teaspoons butter or olive oil**
- **1 cup packaged shredded carrots**
- **½ cup dry white wine or chicken broth**

fabulous focaccia sandwiches

Perfect picnic food in a flash, these hearty sandwiches of juicy rotisserie chicken, herbed mayonnaise, and vegetables on chewy focaccia require only fresh fruit and a bottle of chilled white wine to make an idyllic alfresco meal.

Start to finish: 15 minutes   Makes 4 servings

Using a long serrated knife, cut bread in half horizontally. In a small bowl stir together mayonnaise dressing and basil. Spread cut sides of bread halves with mayonnaise mixture. Layer spinach, chicken, and roasted sweet peppers between bread halves. Cut into quarters.

Nutrition facts per serving: 370 cal., 11 g total fat (4 g sat. fat), 51 mg chol., 148 mg sodium, 43 g carbo., 4 g fiber, 25 g pro. Daily values: 23% vit. A, 94% vit. C, 9% calcium, 13% iron

that's foh-KAH-chee-ah!

Focaccia is a flatbread—akin to deep-dish pizza crust—that originated in the Italian region of Liguria. Olive oil is often incorporated into the dough, as well as being generously brushed on top before the focaccia is finished with the desired toppings, such as minced garlic, onions, fresh herbs, tomatoes, olives, or a dusting of cheese. Generally, the best focaccia is to be found at artisanal or Italian bakeries, but your grocery store might make its own version, too. If you don't plan to eat your focaccia the day it is purchased, place it in a heavy-duty freezer bag and freeze for up to 3 months.

- 1 8- to 10-inch tomato or onion Italian flatbread (focaccia) or 1 loaf sourdough bread
- 3 to 4 tablespoons light mayonnaise dressing
- 1 to 2 tablespoons shredded fresh basil
- 1½ cups packaged prewashed spinach
- 1½ cups sliced or shredded deli-cooked rotisserie chicken
- ½ of a 7-ounce jar roasted red sweet peppers, drained and cut into strips (about ½ cup)

chicken & banana curry

Cultures all over the world love curries. These mélanges of meat, vegetables, and fruit are seasoned with curry powder, a blend of up to 20 spices that can vary greatly in the degree of fire it gives to its namesake dish.

20

8 ounces skinless, boneless chicken thighs or breast halves

¾ cup sliced green onion

3 to 4 teaspoons curry powder

1 tablespoon margarine or butter

¼ cup apricot preserves

⅓ cup mixed dried fruit bits

⅓ cup water

1½ cups plain low-fat yogurt

2 tablespoons cornstarch

1 medium banana, sliced

Hot cooked rice

Start to finish: 20 minutes   Makes 4 servings

Rinse chicken; pat dry. Cut into 1-inch pieces. In a large nonstick skillet cook ½ cup of the green onion and the curry powder in margarine over medium-high heat for 1 minute. Push green onion mixture to side of skillet. Add chicken; cook and stir for 3 to 4 minutes or until no longer pink. Reduce heat.

Snip any large pieces of preserves. Stir preserves, fruit bits, and water into chicken mixture. Stir together yogurt and cornstarch; stir into chicken mixture. Cook and stir until thickened and bubbly. Cook and stir for 2 minutes more.

Stir in banana. Season to taste with salt. Serve over rice and sprinkle with remaining ¼ cup green onion.

Nutrition facts per serving: 374 cal., 8 g total fat (2 g sat. fat), 32 mg chol., 167 mg sodium, 62 g carbo., 1 g fiber, 16 g pro. Daily values: 11% vit. A, 11% vit. C, 15% calcium, 15% iron

jamaican chicken salad

Jerk—pork or chicken flavored with a spice mixture of allspice, thyme, and spicy Scotch bonnet chilies—is as Jamaican as reggae and rum. This savory and sweet salad pairs jerk-seasoned, sautéed chicken with juicy mangoes.

Start to finish: 20 minutes   Makes 4 servings

Rinse chicken; pat dry. Sprinkle both sides of chicken with Jamaican jerk seasoning. In a large skillet cook the seasoned chicken in hot oil over medium heat for 8 to 10 minutes or until tender and no longer pink, turning once.

Meanwhile, for dressing, stir together honey-mustard dressing and lime peel. If necessary, add water to make of drizzling consistency. If using fresh mangoes, pit, peel, and slice.

Divide greens among 4 dinner plates. Thinly bias-slice chicken. Arrange chicken and mangoes on top of greens; drizzle with dressing.

Nutrition facts per serving: 281 cal., 6 g total fat (1 g sat. fat), 59 mg chol., 420 mg sodium, 32 g carbo., 6 g fiber, 25 g pro. Daily values: 59% vit. A, 71% vit. C, 5% calcium, 13% iron

Note: For homemade Jamaican jerk seasoning, combine 1 teaspoon crushed red pepper; 1/2 teaspoon ground allspice; 1/4 teaspoon curry powder; 1/4 teaspoon coarsely ground black pepper; 1/8 teaspoon dried thyme, crushed; 1/8 teaspoon ground red pepper; and 1/8 teaspoon ground ginger.

4 **large skinless, boneless chicken breast halves (1 pound)**

2 **to 3 teaspoons purchased or homemade Jamaican jerk seasoning***

2 **teaspoons cooking oil**

½ **cup bottled fat-free honey-mustard salad dressing**

1 **teaspoon finely shredded lime peel**

16 **chilled refrigerated mango slices in light syrup, drained, or 2 large mangoes**

12 **cups packaged torn mixed salad greens (16 ounces)**

short-order
meat dishes

tuscan lamb chop skillet

Tuscans, once disparaged by the rest of Italy as "bean eaters" because of their love of the legume, now wear that mantle with pride. Here, healthful white beans are flavored with rosemary and garlic, then topped with lamb chops.

23

Start to finish: 18 minutes   Makes 4 servings

Trim fat from chops. In a large skillet cook chops in hot oil over medium heat about 8 minutes for medium doneness, turning once. Transfer chops to a plate; keep warm.

Stir garlic into drippings in skillet. Cook and stir for 1 minute. Stir in beans, undrained tomatoes, vinegar, and snipped rosemary. Bring to boiling; reduce heat. Simmer, uncovered, for 3 minutes.

Spoon bean mixture onto 4 dinner plates; arrange 2 chops on each serving. If desired, garnish with rosemary sprigs.

Nutrition facts per serving: 272 cal., 9 g total fat (3 g sat. fat), 67 mg chol., 466 mg sodium, 24 g carbo., 6 g fiber, 30 g pro. Daily values: 4% vit. A, 13% vit. C, 4% calcium, 21% iron

8 lamb rib chops, cut 1 inch thick
   (1½ pounds)

2 teaspoons olive oil

3 cloves garlic, minced

1 19-ounce can white kidney
   (cannellini) beans, rinsed
   and drained

1 8-ounce can Italian-style
   stewed tomatoes, undrained

1 tablespoon balsamic vinegar

2 teaspoons snipped fresh rosemary

   Fresh rosemary sprigs (optional)

bistro beef & mushrooms

Serve French bistro fare in a flash. The Burgundian flavors of Dijon mustard, red wine, and fresh thyme spark this hearty dish. Accompany the steaks with deli mashed potatoes and steamed and buttered *haricots verts* (tiny, slender green beans).

24

4 beef tenderloin steaks, cut
   ¾ inch thick (1 pound)

1 tablespoon Dijon-style mustard
   or coarse-grain brown mustard

2 tablespoons olive oil or roasted
   garlic olive oil

2 4-ounce packages sliced
   crimini, shiitake, or portobello
   mushrooms or one 8-ounce
   package sliced button
   mushrooms (about 3 cups)

⅓ cup dry red wine or sherry

1 tablespoon white wine
   Worcestershire sauce

2 teaspoons snipped fresh thyme

Start to finish: 20 minutes   Makes 4 servings

Trim fat from steaks. Spread mustard evenly over both sides of steaks. In a large skillet heat 1 tablespoon of the oil over medium heat. Add steaks; cook to desired doneness, turning once. (Allow 7 to 10 minutes for medium rare or 10 to 12 minutes for medium.) Transfer steaks to a serving platter; keep warm.

Add remaining 1 tablespoon oil to drippings in skillet. Add mushrooms; cook and stir for 4 minutes. Stir in wine, Worcestershire sauce, and thyme. Simmer, uncovered, for 3 minutes. Spoon over steaks.

Nutrition facts per serving: 263 cal., 14 g total fat (4 g sat. fat), 64 mg chol., 176 mg sodium, 5 g carbo., 1 g fiber, 23 g pro. Daily values: 0% vit. A, 4% vit. C, 1% calcium, 25% iron

red-pepper
steak linguine

Meet the new pepper steak. This delicious dish has nuances of that hearty classic, but has been freshened up with pasta, pea pods, and an enticing red-pepper sauce—and made speedy with deli-roasted beef tenderloin.

Start to finish: 18 minutes   Makes 3 servings

Cook pasta according to package directions, adding pea pods to pasta the last 2 minutes of cooking. Drain and keep warm.

Meanwhile, cut beef into bite-size pieces; set aside. For sauce, place roasted sweet peppers in a food processor bowl or blender container; cover and process or blend until finely chopped. Add sour cream, salsa, flour, and sugar; cover and process until nearly smooth. Transfer sauce to a small saucepan.

Stir milk into sauce. Cook and stir over medium heat until slightly thickened and bubbly. Cook and stir for 1 minute more. Stir in beef; heat through. Spoon sauce over pasta.

Nutrition facts per serving: 460 cal., 13 g total fat (4 g sat. fat), 67 mg chol., 140 mg sodium,
58 g carbo., 2 g fiber, 29 g pro. Daily values: 30% vit. A, 267% vit. C, 7% calcium, 32% iron

1 **9-ounce package refrigerated linguine or fettuccine**

1 **cup fresh pea pods (4 ounces)**

6 **ounces deli-roasted beef tenderloin sliced ¼ inch thick**

1 **7-ounce jar roasted red sweet peppers, rinsed and drained (about 1 cup)**

¼ **cup light dairy sour cream**

2 **tablespoons salsa**

1½ **teaspoons all-purpose flour**

½ **teaspoon sugar**

½ **cup milk**

beef with cucumber raita

In the oft-fiery cuisine of India, a respite is offered in the form of a raita, a simple, cooling salad made with yogurt and fruits or vegetables. Snipped mint makes this raita particularly flavorful and refreshing.

Start to finish: 20 minutes   Makes 4 servings

Preheat gas grill* or broiler. For raita, in a small bowl combine yogurt, cucumber, onion, snipped mint, and sugar. Season to taste with salt and pepper; set aside.

Trim fat from steak. Sprinkle steak with lemon-pepper seasoning. Grill steak on the rack of an uncovered grill directly over medium heat or broil for 12 to 15 minutes for medium doneness, turning once. Cut steak across the grain into thin slices. If desired, arrange steak slices on mint leaves. Top with raita.

Nutrition facts per serving: 237 cal., 10 g total fat (4 g sat. fat), 77 mg chol., 235 mg sodium, 5 g carbo., 0 g fiber, 29 g pro. Daily values: 1% vit. A, 3% vit. C, 10% calcium, 21% iron

Note: Charcoal grill may be used, but allow extra time for coals to reach proper temperature.

1   8-ounce carton plain fat-free or low-fat yogurt

¼   cup coarsely shredded unpeeled cucumber

1   tablespoon finely chopped red or sweet onion

1   tablespoon snipped fresh mint

¼   teaspoon sugar

1   pound boneless beef sirloin steak, cut 1 inch thick

½   teaspoon lemon-pepper seasoning

Fresh mint leaves (optional)

beef & sweet onion sandwiches

With sirloin strips instead of ground beef, mustard-sauced sautéed onion, and crisp and colorful vegetables, these beef sandwiches have a definite edge on elegance over hamburgers—and they're just as easy to make.

12 ounces boneless beef sirloin or top round steak, cut 1 inch thick

½ teaspoon coarsely ground black pepper

2 teaspoons cooking oil

1 medium sweet onion (such as Vidalia or Walla Walla), sliced

2 tablespoons Dijon-style mustard

½ of a 7-ounce jar roasted red sweet peppers, drained (about ½ cup)

8 1-inch-thick slices sourdough or marbled rye bread

1½ cups torn packaged prewashed spinach or other salad greens

Start to finish: 20 minutes   Makes 4 servings

Trim fat from steak. Sprinkle both sides of steak with black pepper; press in lightly. In a large skillet cook steak in hot oil over medium-high heat about 8 minutes or until slightly pink in center, turning once. Remove from skillet; keep warm. Add onion to drippings in skillet. (Add more oil, if necessary.) Cook and stir about 5 minutes or until onion is crisp-tender. Stir in mustard; remove from heat.

Meanwhile, cut roasted sweet peppers into ½-inch-wide strips. Toast bread, if desired, and shred spinach.

Just before serving, cut steak into bite-size strips. To serve, top 4 bread slices with spinach, steak strips, roasted pepper strips, onion mixture, and remaining bread slices.

Nutrition facts per serving: 335 cal., 12 g total fat (4 g sat. fat), 57 mg chol., 553 mg sodium, 30 g carbo., 1 g fiber, 25 g pro. Daily values: 23% vit. A, 96% vit. C, 5% calcium, 28% iron

moo shu-style beef
& cabbage wraps

Dig in to moo shu made easy. Similar in taste and preparation to the filled Chinese rice pancakes, these wraps use ground beef, preshredded vegetables, and warm tortillas to make quick work of a satisfying dinner.

Start to finish: 20 minutes   Makes 4 servings

Wrap tortillas in foil. Heat in a 350° oven for 10 minutes to soften. Meanwhile, for filling, in a large skillet cook ground beef and onion until meat is no longer pink; drain well. Stir in cabbage and corn. Cook, covered, about 4 minutes or until vegetables are tender, stirring once. Stir in the ¼ cup hoisin sauce and the sesame oil. Cook and stir until heated through.

Spoon ½ cup filling onto each tortilla just below center. Fold bottom edge up and over filling. Fold opposite sides in, just until they meet. Roll up from bottom. If desired, serve with additional hoisin sauce.

Nutrition facts per serving: 431 cal., 14 g total fat (5 g sat. fat), 54 mg chol., 604 mg sodium, 52 g carbo., 4 g fiber, 21 g pro. Daily values: 20% vit. A, 37% vit. C, 7% calcium, 25% iron

8 8-inch flour tortillas

12 ounces lean ground beef

½ cup chopped red or green onion

2 cups packaged shredded
    cabbage with carrot
    (cole slaw mix)

1 cup fresh cut corn or frozen
    whole kernel corn

¼ cup hoisin sauce

1 teaspoon toasted sesame oil

    Hoisin sauce (optional)

sweet and tangy hoisin

Hoisin (HOY-sin) sauce is a sweet, slightly tongue-tingling sauce with a distinctive flavor that comes from fermented soybeans, molasses, vinegar, mustard, sesame seed, garlic, and chilies. It makes a nice sauce for just about any Asian stir-fry or can fill in as a change-of-pace barbecue sauce. In most grocery stores, look for hoisin sauce alongside the soy sauce. If you can't find it, try an Asian market.

flank steak with pineapple salsa

The fresh-tasting fruit salsa that enlivens this warm steak salad starts with green picante sauce. Just add pineapple, sweet peppers, and mandarin oranges—and serve.

2 cups chopped peeled and cored fresh pineapple

1 11-ounce can mandarin orange sections, drained

½ cup chopped red or green sweet pepper

⅓ cup mild green picante sauce or green taco sauce

12 ounces beef flank or boneless sirloin steak, cut ½ inch thick

½ teaspoon Mexican seasoning or chili powder

1 tablespoon olive oil

4 to 6 cups packaged torn mixed salad greens

Start to finish: 20 minutes   Makes 4 servings

For pineapple salsa, in a medium bowl gently stir together pineapple, mandarin oranges, sweet pepper, and picante sauce. Set aside.

Trim fat from steak. Thinly slice steak across the grain. Sprinkle with Mexican seasoning; toss to coat evenly. In a large skillet cook and stir half of the seasoned steak in hot oil over medium-high heat for 2 to 3 minutes or to desired doneness. Remove from skillet. Repeat with remaining steak.

Arrange salad greens on plates. Top with steak and pineapple salsa.

Nutrition facts per serving: 245 cal., 10 g total fat (3 g sat. fat), 40 mg chol., 224 mg sodium, 23 g carbo., 2 g fiber, 18 g pro. Daily values: 21% vit. A, 67% vit. C, 2% calcium, 16% iron

jamaican pork & sweet potato stir-fry

Take a vacation from the postwork, predinner rush with this Jamaica-inspired dish that features two of this easygoing island's favorite ingredients: lean pork and golden sweet potatoes. For flavor, pick up Jamaican jerk seasoning in the grocery store spice aisle.

Start to finish: 18 minutes   Makes 4 servings

Prepare rice according to package directions. Stir half of the green onion into cooked rice. Meanwhile, peel sweet potato. Cut in quarters lengthwise, then thinly slice crosswise.* Place in a microwave-safe pie plate or shallow dish. Cover with vented plastic wrap. Microwave on 100% power (high) for 3 to 4 minutes or until tender, stirring once. Cut apple into 16 wedges. Sprinkle pork strips with Jamaican jerk seasoning; toss to coat evenly.

Pour oil into a wok or large skillet. (Add more oil, if necessary, during cooking.) Preheat over medium-high heat. Stir-fry seasoned pork in hot oil for 2 minutes. Add apple and remaining green onion; stir-fry for 1 to 2 minutes or until pork is no longer pink. Stir in sweet potato and apple juice. Bring to boiling; reduce heat. Simmer, uncovered, for 1 minute more. Serve over rice mixture.

Nutrition facts per serving: 365 cal., 9 g total fat (2 g sat. fat), 38 mg chol., 131 mg sodium, 54 g carbo., 3 g fiber, 16 g pro. Daily values: 150% vit. A, 32% vit. C, 3% calcium, 17% iron

*Note: To save time, slice quartered sweet potato (and the green onion) in a food processor fitted with a thin slicing blade.

- 1½ cups quick-cooking rice
- ¼ cup thinly sliced green onion
- 1 large sweet potato (about 12 ounces)
- 1 medium tart apple (such as Granny Smith), cored
- 12 ounces lean boneless pork strips for stir-frying
- 2 to 3 teaspoons purchased or homemade Jamaican jerk seasoning (see page 21)
- 1 tablespoon cooking oil
- ⅓ cup apple juice or water

pork medallions
with cherry sauce

During the autumn months, pork is often prepared with fruit such as prunes or apples. These quick-seared medallions cloaked in a delightful sweet cherry sauce provide a whole new reason—and season—to pair pork with fruit.

Start to finish: 20 minutes   Makes 4 servings

Trim fat from pork. Cut pork crosswise into 1-inch-thick slices. Place each slice between 2 pieces of plastic wrap. With the heel of your hand, press each slice into a ½-inch-thick medallion. Remove plastic wrap. Sprinkle lightly with salt and freshly ground black pepper.

Spray an unheated large nonstick skillet with nonstick coating. Heat skillet over medium-high heat. Add pork; cook for 6 minutes or until pork is slightly pink in center and juices run clear, turning once. Transfer to a serving platter; keep warm.

Combine cranberry juice, mustard, and cornstarch; add to skillet. Cook and stir until thickened and bubbly. Cook and stir for 2 minutes more. Stir cherries into mixture in skillet. Serve over pork.

Nutrition facts per serving: 197 cal., 5 g total fat (2 g sat. fat), 81 mg chol., 127 mg sodium, 12 g carbo., 0 g fiber, 26 g pro. Daily values: 0% vit. A, 31% vit. C, 1% calcium, 10% iron

1 **pound pork tenderloin**

Nonstick spray coating

¾ **cup cranberry juice cocktail or apple juice**

2 **teaspoons spicy brown mustard**

1 **teaspoon cornstarch**

1 **cup sweet cherries (such as Rainier or Bing), halved and pitted, or 1 cup frozen unsweetened pitted dark sweet cherries, thawed**

coyote pizza

A chili-spiced pork sausage called chorizo, fresh Mexican cheese, and blazing hot pepper (if you so choose) give Southwestern flair to this quick-to-fix pizza.

8 ounces bulk chorizo or Italian sausage, casings removed

1 12-inch Italian bread shell (Boboli)

⅔ cup refrigerated or bottled roasted red sweet pepper sauce

¼ cup sliced green onion

⅔ cup crumbled or shredded queso fresco cheese* and/or Monterey Jack cheese (2½ ounces)

2 plum tomatoes, thinly sliced

½ cup light dairy sour cream (optional)

Fresh serrano or jalapeño pepper, thinly sliced (optional)

Start to finish: 20 minutes   Makes 6 servings

In a medium skillet cook sausage until meat is no longer pink; drain well. Meanwhile, place bread shell on a 12-inch pizza pan. Spread with roasted sweet pepper sauce. Bake in a 425° oven for 5 minutes.

Top with cooked sausage and green onion; sprinkle with cheese. Bake about 5 minutes more or until heated through. Top with tomato slices. If desired, add sour cream and sliced serrano pepper.

Nutrition facts per serving: 267 cal., 23 g total fat (7 g sat. fat), 14 mg chol., 651 mg sodium, 38 g carbo., 2 g fiber, 21 g pro. Daily values: 9% vit. A, 16% vit. C, 11% calcium, 12% iron

Note: Queso fresco is a mildly salty white Mexican cheese found in supermarkets or Mexican groceries.

great meals by the slice

If pizza still means pepperoni, tomato sauce, and cheese at your house, consider a change of taste. Start with an Italian bread shell as a base and the ingredient combinations are endless. For sauce, spread on a flavored tomato or alfredo pasta sauce or a thin layer of pesto. Sauté a mix of your favorite vegetables and garlic in olive oil as a topper. Cooked shrimp, sautéed chicken, marinated artichoke hearts, steamed asparagus, pitted Greek olives, and feta or goat cheese also make tasty toppings.

ham with five-spice vegetables

Salty ham, sweet and crunchy sugar snap peas, and an aromatic five-spice blend of star anise, ginger, cinnamon, cloves, and Szechwan peppercorns make a delicious all-in-one dinner that touches on nearly all of the taste sensations.

Start to finish: 20 minutes   Makes 4 servings

In a covered medium saucepan cook carrots in a small amount of boiling water for 5 minutes. Add snap peas and broccoli; return to boiling. Cook, covered, 2 minutes more or until vegetables are crisp-tender; drain.

Meanwhile, trim fat from ham. Cut ham into 4 serving-size pieces. In a large skillet cook ham in hot oil over medium heat until heated through, turning once. Transfer ham to a serving platter; keep warm. Stir five-spice powder into drippings in skillet. Stir in honey and soy sauce. Bring to boiling. Gently stir in cooked vegetables; heat through. Spoon vegetable mixture over ham.

Nutrition facts per serving: 209 cal., 6 g total fat (2 g sat. fat), 45 mg chol., 1,212 mg sodium, 17 g carbo., 5 g fiber, 21 g pro. Daily values: 176% vit. A, 103% vit. C, 5% calcium, 19% iron

4 **medium carrots, sliced (2 cups)**

1 **cup fresh or frozen sugar snap peas**

1 **cup packaged shredded broccoli (broccoli slaw mix)**

¾ **to 1 pound lower-fat cooked center-cut ham slice**

1 **teaspoon cooking oil**

½ **teaspoon five-spice powder**

1 **tablespoon honey**

1 **tablespoon reduced-sodium soy sauce**

weeknight
fish & seafood

poached orange roughy
with lemon sauce

Despite its speed, poaching is an inherently gentle way to cook. It's also one of the lightest and most healthful. Here, poaching in lemon- and pepper-infused broth preserves the delicate flavor and texture of one of the most popular kinds of white fish.

Start to finish: 20 minutes   Makes 4 servings

Rinse fish; pat dry. Cut fish into 4 serving-size pieces; set aside. Snap off and discard woody bases from asparagus. Cut asparagus in half; set aside.

In a 10-inch skillet combine 1 cup of the broth, the lemon peel, and black pepper. Bring to boiling; reduce heat. Carefully add the fish and asparagus. Cook, covered, over medium-low heat for 4 minutes. Add sweet pepper strips. Cook, covered, 2 minutes more or until fish flakes easily with a fork. Using a slotted spatula, transfer fish and vegetables to a serving platter, reserving liquid in skillet. Keep fish and vegetables warm.

For sauce, stir together remaining broth and cornstarch. Stir into liquid in skillet. Cook and stir until thickened and bubbly. Cook and stir for 2 minutes more. Stir in chives. Arrange fish and vegetables on couscous; top with sauce.

Nutrition facts per serving: 249 cal., 2 g total fat (0 g sat. fat), 60 mg chol., 390 mg sodium, 29 g carbo., 6 g fiber, 28 g pro. Daily values: 8% vit. A, 96% vit. C, 3% calcium, 8% iron

1 **pound fresh orange roughy or red snapper, ½ inch thick**

1 **pound asparagus spears**

1 **14½-ounce can reduced-sodium chicken broth**

2 **teaspoons finely shredded lemon peel**

⅛ **teaspoon black pepper**

1 **medium yellow sweet pepper, cut into bite-size strips**

4 **teaspoons cornstarch**

2 **tablespoons snipped fresh chives**

2 **cups hot cooked couscous or rice**

red snapper veracruz

Once a part of New Spain, Veracruz resides on the Gulf of Mexico and is famous for its seafood, most notably for its namesake specialty. The traditional accompaniment to Red Snapper Veracruz is boiled potatoes—but quick-cooking couscous is far faster.

40

⅓ cup salsa

1 clove garlic, minced

1 14½-ounce can vegetable broth

1 cup quick-cooking couscous

¼ cup thinly sliced green onion or coarsely chopped fresh cilantro

4 4-ounce fresh skinless red snapper or orange roughy fillets, ½ to 1 inch thick

Lime or lemon wedges

Start to finish: 15 minutes   Makes 4 servings

Preheat broiler. Combine salsa and garlic; set aside. In a medium saucepan bring broth to boiling. Stir in couscous; cover and remove from heat. Let stand about 5 minutes or until liquid is absorbed. Stir in green onion.

Meanwhile, rinse fish; pat dry. Place fish on the greased unheated rack of a broiler pan. Broil about 4 inches from the heat until fish flakes easily with a fork (allow 4 to 6 minutes per ½-inch thickness of fish). Turn 1-inch-thick fillets over halfway through broiling. Spoon the salsa mixture over fish; broil 1 minute more or until salsa is heated through.

Arrange fish on couscous mixture. Serve with lime wedges.

Nutrition facts per serving: 295 cal., 3 g total fat (0 g sat. fat), 42 mg chol., 549 mg sodium, 39 g carbo., 7 g fiber, 30 g pro. Daily values: 4% vit. A, 12% vit. C, 4% calcium, 7% iron

cuban-style sea bass

A chili pepper-spiced pineapple and black bean salsa is a fitting accompaniment to this Cuban-style fish dish featuring tender fillets of sea bass. Whip up a homemade mango milk shake for dessert.

Start to finish: 18 minutes   Makes 4 servings

Preheat gas grill* or broiler. Combine the beans, pineapple, jalapeño pepper, marmalade, and vinegar. If desired, transfer to a small saucepan, then cook and stir over medium heat until heated through.

Rinse fish; pat dry. Brush fish with soy sauce. Grill fish on the greased rack of an uncovered grill directly over medium heat or broil until fish flakes easily with a fork (allow 4 to 6 minutes per ½-inch thickness of fish). Turn 1-inch-thick fillets over halfway through cooking. To serve, arrange fish on pineapple and black bean salsa. Sprinkle with onion.

Nutrition facts per serving: 218 cal., 3 g total fat (1 g sat. fat), 47 mg chol., 474 mg sodium, 25 g carbo., 6 g fiber, 28 g pro. Daily values: 5% vit. A, 20% vit. C, 4% calcium, 11% iron

Note: Charcoal grill may be used, but allow extra time for coals to reach proper temperature.

hot, hot, hot peppers
Because all chili peppers contain oils that can burn your eyes, lips, and skin, protect yourself when working with them by covering your hands with plastic bags. Wash your hands thoroughly before touching your face.

- 1 15-ounce can black beans, rinsed and drained
- ½ cup chopped fresh pineapple
- 1 fresh jalapeño or serrano pepper, seeded and finely chopped
- 2 tablespoons orange or lime marmalade
- 2 tablespoons seasoned rice vinegar or white wine vinegar
- 4 4-ounce fresh sea bass fillets, ½ to 1 inch thick
- 1 tablespoon reduced-sodium soy sauce
- 2 tablespoons finely chopped red onion

honey-glazed tuna & greens

Here's fusion cuisine—a hybrid of Asian and European cooking—made fast. As the tuna is quick-grilled to seal in the juices, a soy-honey sauce with a touch of heat from crushed red pepper caramelizes, creating a beautiful and delicious glaze.

42

¼ cup honey

¼ cup reduced-sodium soy sauce

1 teaspoon toasted sesame oil

½ teaspoon crushed red pepper

4 5-ounce fresh tuna steaks, ½ to 1 inch thick

12 cups packaged mesclun or torn mixed bitter salad greens (about 8 ounces)

10 to 12 pear-shaped yellow or red cherry tomatoes, halved

Start to finish: 20 minutes   Makes 4 servings

Preheat gas grill* or broiler. In a small bowl combine honey, soy sauce, oil, and red pepper. Set aside 2 tablespoons to brush on the fish and reserve remaining for dressing.

Rinse fish; pat dry. Brush both sides of fish with the 2 tablespoons soy mixture. Grill fish on the greased rack of an uncovered grill directly over medium heat or broil until fish flakes easily with a fork (allow 4 to 6 minutes per ½-inch thickness of fish). Turn 1-inch-thick steaks over halfway through cooking.

Toss together mesclun and tomatoes; arrange on 4 dinner plates. Cut tuna across the grain into ½-inch-wide slices; arrange on greens. Drizzle with reserved soy mixture.

Nutrition facts per serving: 279 cal., 2 g total fat (0 g sat. fat), 24 mg chol., 1,015 mg sodium, 22 g carbo., 1 g fiber, 42 g pro. Daily values: 9% vit. A, 21% vit. C, 2% calcium, 35% iron

Note: Charcoal grill may be used, but allow extra time for coals to reach proper temperature.

salmon caesar salad

Salad in a bag just about sums up culinary convenience (someone else did the washing and tearing for you). A few additions to always-popular Caesar salad turn it into a gourmet main dish.

1 10-ounce package Caesar salad
   (includes lettuce, dressing,
   croutons, and cheese)*
1 small yellow, red, or green sweet
   pepper, cut into thin strips
1 small cucumber, quartered
   lengthwise and sliced
6 ounces smoked, poached, or
   canned salmon, skinned, boned,
   and broken into chunks (1 cup)
½ of a lemon, cut into 3 wedges

Start to finish: 15 minutes   Makes 3 servings

In a large salad bowl combine the lettuce and dressing from packaged salad, sweet pepper strips, and cucumber; toss gently to coat. Add salmon and the croutons and cheese from packaged salad; toss gently to mix. Divide among 3 dinner plates. Before serving, squeeze juice from a lemon wedge over each salad.

Nutrition facts per serving: 199 cal., 11 g total fat (1 g sat. fat), 16 mg chol., 564 mg sodium, 10 g carbo., 2 g fiber, 14 g pro. Daily values: 25% vit. A, 69% vit. C, 8% calcium, 9% iron

Note: If you can't find packaged Caesar salad, substitute 5 cups torn mixed salad greens, ⅓ cup croutons, 3 tablespoons bottled Caesar or ranch salad dressing, and 2 tablespoons grated Parmesan cheese.

poached to perfection

To poach salmon, rinse 8 ounces fresh salmon fillets; pat dry. In a large skillet bring 1¾ cups water to boiling; add salmon. Simmer, covered, until fish flakes easily with a fork (allow 4 to 6 minutes per ½-inch thickness of fish). Yields about 6 ounces poached salmon.

salmon scallops with tarragon cream

Elegance has a light side. Here, tender salmon fillets or steaks are cut into coin-size scallops, quick-fried, then coated with a silky, low-fat cream sauce infused with fresh herbs. Serve it all over pasta and zucchini.

Start to finish: 20 minutes   Makes 3 servings

Cook pasta according to package directions, adding zucchini to pasta the last 1 minute of cooking. Drain and keep warm. Meanwhile, skin fish, if necessary. Rinse fish; pat dry. Cut into 1-inch pieces.

In a large nonstick skillet cook and stir fish in hot oil over medium-high heat for 3 to 5 minutes or until fish flakes easily with a fork. Remove from skillet. Add milk, cream cheese, tarragon, and pepper to skillet. Cook and whisk until cream cheese is melted and sauce is smooth. Return salmon to skillet. Cook and stir gently until heated through. Serve over fettuccine and zucchini.

Nutrition facts per serving: 434 cal., 13 g total fat (4 g sat. fat), 50 mg chol., 169 mg sodium, 51 g carbo., 1 g fiber, 29 g pro. Daily values: 12% vit. A, 7% vit. C, 8% calcium, 15% iron

1 **9-ounce package refrigerated fettuccine**

2 **cups thinly sliced zucchini, yellow summer squash, and/or red sweet pepper**

12 **ounces fresh salmon fillets or steaks**

1 **teaspoon cooking oil**

⅔ **cup low-fat milk**

3 **tablespoons reduced-fat cream cheese (Neufchâtel)**

1 **tablespoon snipped fresh tarragon, basil, or dill**

¼ **teaspoon pepper**

pan-seared scallops

This is a flash in the pan! Sweet scallops are given a Cajun-flavored crust, then tossed with balsamic vinegar-dressed spinach and crisp-cooked bacon. Serve with corn bread and cold beer and you have a meal that's both homey and elegant in no time flat.

Start to finish: 20 minutes   Makes 4 servings

Rinse scallops; pat dry. In a plastic bag combine flour and seasoning. Add scallops; toss to coat. In a large skillet cook scallops in hot oil over medium heat about 6 minutes or until browned and opaque, turning once. Remove scallops.

Add spinach to skillet; sprinkle with water. Cook, covered, over medium-high heat 2 minutes or until spinach is wilted. Add vinegar; toss to coat evenly. Return scallops; heat through. Sprinkle with bacon.

Nutrition facts per serving: 158 cal., 6 g total fat (1 g sat. fat), 37 mg chol., 323 mg sodium, 9 g carbo., 2 g fiber, 18 g pro. Daily values: 49% vit. A, 37% vit. C, 12% calcium, 29% iron

- 1 **pound fresh sea scallops**
- 2 **tablespoons all-purpose flour**
- 1 **to 2 teaspoons blackened steak seasoning or Cajun seasoning**
- 1 **tablespoon cooking oil**
- 1 **10-ounce package prewashed spinach**
- 1 **tablespoon water**
- 2 **tablespoons balsamic vinegar**
- ¼ **cup cooked bacon pieces**

buy-the-sea scallops

As suggested by their name, sea scallops are the larger of the two most widely available varieties of this kind of shellfish. Bay scallops, the smaller variety, have a sweet flavor similar to sea scallops. Scallops should be firm, sweet smelling, and free of excess cloudy liquid. Chill shucked scallops covered with their own liquid in a closed container for up to 2 days.

paella-style shrimp & couscous

Save time-consuming Spanish paella—made with saffron, seafood, and rice—for a weekend cooking adventure. As a quick weeknight dish, consider this curried version, made with colorful vegetables, curry powder, and couscous.

48

1   14½-ounce can chicken broth

1   teaspoon curry powder

¼   teaspoon bottled hot pepper sauce

1   12-ounce package frozen peeled
     and deveined shrimp

1   cup quick-cooking couscous

1   6- or 6½-ounce jar marinated
     artichoke hearts, drained
     and coarsely chopped

¾   cup frozen peas

1   cup cherry tomatoes

Start to finish: 18 minutes   Makes 4 servings

In a large saucepan bring broth, curry powder, and pepper sauce to boiling. Add the frozen shrimp. Return just to boiling; reduce heat. Simmer, uncovered, for 1 to 3 minutes or until shrimp turn pink.

Stir in couscous, artichoke hearts, and peas. Cover; remove from heat. Let stand about 5 minutes or until liquid is absorbed. Meanwhile, halve tomatoes. Stir tomatoes into shrimp mixture.

Nutrition facts per serving: 321 cal., 5 g total fat (0 g sat. fat), 131 mg chol., 639 mg sodium, 46 g carbo., 9 g fiber, 24 g pro. Daily values: 13% vit. A, 40% vit. C, 5% calcium, 25% iron

hoisin shrimp & pineapple

In the mood for *South Pacific?* This sweet and savory combination of shrimp, pineapple, and sweet peppers served over rice fills the bill—and leaves time after dinner to watch the movie, too.

Start to finish: 20 minutes   Makes 4 servings

Thaw shrimp, if frozen. Rinse shrimp; pat dry. Drain pineapple, reserving ¼ cup juice. Set pineapple aside. Combine reserved pineapple juice and hoisin sauce.

For sauce, in a small bowl combine ¼ cup of the hoisin-pineapple juice mixture, the apricot preserves, and lemon juice; set aside. In a large bowl combine shrimp, pineapple, sweet pepper, and remaining hoisin-pineapple juice mixture; toss gently to coat. Drain shrimp mixture, discarding excess liquid.

Place shrimp, pineapple, and sweet pepper pieces on the unheated rack of a broiler pan. Broil 3 to 4 inches from the heat for 6 to 8 minutes or until shrimp turn pink. Spoon rice onto a serving platter; top with shrimp, pineapple, and sweet pepper. Sprinkle with cilantro. Drizzle with reserved sauce.

Nutrition facts per serving: 257 cal., 2 g total fat (0 g sat. fat), 131 mg chol., 609 mg sodium, 44 g carbo., 2 g fiber, 16 g pro. Daily values: 23% vit. A, 93% vit. C, 3% calcium, 17% iron

12 ounces fresh or frozen peeled and deveined large shrimp

1½ cups purchased fresh pineapple chunks (packed in juice)

¼ cup hoisin sauce

3 tablespoons apricot preserves

1 tablespoon lemon juice

1 large red, orange, or green sweet pepper, cut into 1-inch pieces

3 cups hot cooked quick-cooking brown rice

1 tablespoon snipped fresh cilantro or sliced green onion

great
pasta plates

trattoria-style
spinach fettuccine

This fettuccine special is just the kind of soulful pasta dish that neighborhood trattorias take pride in serving. It tosses an intensely flavored double-tomato sauce with tangy feta cheese for a dinner that deserves a red-checked tablecloth and candles.

Start to finish: 18 minutes   Makes 4 servings

Using kitchen scissors, cut fettuccine strands in half. Cook the pasta according to package directions; drain. Return pasta to hot pan.

Meanwhile, in a large skillet cook shallot in hot oil over medium heat for 30 seconds. Stir in fresh tomatoes, carrot, and dried tomatoes. Cook, covered, for 5 minutes, stirring once. Spoon tomato mixture over cooked pasta; toss gently. Sprinkle individual servings with cheese.

Nutrition facts per serving: 311 cal., 11 g total fat (4 g sat. fat), 73 mg chol., 250 mg sodium, 44 g carbo., 2 g fiber, 13 g pro. Daily values: 61% vit. A, 48% vit. C, 10% calcium, 23% iron

1 **9-ounce package refrigerated spinach fettuccine**

2 **tablespoons chopped shallot or green onion**

1 **tablespoon olive oil**

4 **red and/or yellow tomatoes, chopped (2 cups)**

1 **medium carrot, finely chopped**

¼ **cup oil-packed dried tomatoes, drained and snipped**

½ **cup crumbled garlic and herb or peppercorn feta cheese (2 ounces)**

mixed herb pasta salad

Good taste doesn't get any fresher than pasta tossed with tangy salad greens and a whole host of fresh herbs, then dressed simply with olive oil, lemon juice, salt, and pepper. It's a veritable herb garden on a plate.

1   9-ounce package refrigerated angel hair pasta or linguine

3   cups packaged mesclun or torn mixed salad greens

12   to 15 cherry tomatoes, halved

¾   cup lightly packed fresh basil and/or Italian parsley, snipped

¼   cup lightly packed fresh tarragon, savory, oregano, thyme, and/or chives, snipped

2   to 3 tablespoons olive oil

½   of a lemon, cut into 3 wedges

Start to finish: 20 minutes   Makes 3 servings

Using kitchen scissors, cut pasta strands in half. Cook pasta according to package directions. Drain in colander. Rinse with cold water; drain again. Transfer to a large bowl.

Add mesclun, tomatoes, and herbs to pasta. Drizzle with enough oil to coat, tossing gently. Season to taste with salt. Divide among 3 dinner plates. Season with pepper, if desired. Before serving, squeeze juice from a lemon wedge over each salad.

Nutrition facts per serving: 346 cal., 12 g total fat (1 g sat. fat), 15 mg chol., 71 mg sodium, 51 g carbo., 1 g fiber, 11 g pro. Daily values: 6% vit. A, 31% vit. C, 3% calcium, 11% iron

lettuce spice up your salads

Mesclun has hit the mainstream! This French mixture of tiny greens that may include peppery arugula, chervil, chickweed, dandelion, and oak leaf lettuce was once considered to be solely the domain of the gourmet, but now is often available at large supermarkets. Its greatest boon is flavor; unlike the mildly flavored iceberg, these spicy herblike greens together have a distinct taste, which is nicely accented by a drizzle of vinaigrette.

capellini with shrimp in pesto sauce

It's said that sailors from the Italian port city of Genoa popularized pesto—the aromatic sauce of fresh basil, garlic, olive oil, Parmesan cheese, and pine nuts. Pesto has the earthy, green freshness they undoubtedly yearned for on their long journeys.

53

Start to finish: 20 minutes   Makes 4 servings

Thaw shrimp, if frozen. Rinse shrimp; pat dry. Cook pasta according to package directions. Drain and keep warm.

Meanwhile, spray an unheated large nonstick skillet with nonstick coating (or, brush with a little oil drained from pesto). Heat skillet over medium-high heat. Add shrimp; cook and stir for 2 minutes. Add squash; cook and stir about 2 minutes more or until shrimp turn pink and squash is crisp-tender. Remove skillet from heat. Add pesto; toss gently to coat.

Serve shrimp mixture over pasta; sprinkle with tomato.

Nutrition facts per serving: 428 cal., 16 g total fat (0 g sat. fat), 134 mg chol., 316 mg sodium, 47 g carbo., 3 g fiber, 25 g pro. Daily values: 16% vit. A, 13% vit. C, 4% calcium, 30% iron

12 ounces fresh or frozen peeled and deveined shrimp

8 ounces dried tomato-flavored angel hair pasta (capellini), fettuccine, or linguine

Nonstick spray coating

2 medium yellow summer squash and/or zucchini, cut into ½-inch chunks (about 2 cups)

⅓ cup purchased pesto

1 medium plum tomato, chopped

rotini & sweet pepper primavera

Primavera means spring in Italian. This creamy pasta punctuated with tender asparagus, crisp sweet peppers, and tiny baby squash is the essence of that welcome season.

Start to finish: 20 minutes   Makes 4 servings

Snap off and discard woody bases from asparagus. Bias-slice asparagus into 1-inch pieces (about 1½ cups).

Cook pasta according to package directions, adding asparagus, sweet pepper, and squash to pasta the last 3 minutes of cooking; drain. Return pasta and vegetables to hot pan.

Meanwhile, in a small saucepan combine alfredo sauce, tarragon, and crushed red pepper. Cook and stir over medium heat about 5 minutes or until mixture is heated through. Pour over pasta and vegetables; toss gently to coat.

Nutrition facts per serving: 421 cal., 12 g total fat (6 g sat. fat), 31 mg chol., 622 mg sodium, 66 g carbo., 2 g fiber, 15 g pro. Daily values: 29% vit. A, 84% vit. C, 16% calcium, 18% iron

14 **ounces asparagus spears**

8 **ounces dried rotini or gemelli pasta (about 2½ cups)**

1 **cup mixed sweet pepper chunks from salad bar or 1 large red or yellow sweet pepper, cut into 1-inch pieces**

1 **cup halved baby pattypan squash or sliced yellow summer squash**

1 **10-ounce container refrigerated light alfredo sauce**

2 **tablespoons snipped fresh tarragon or thyme**

¼ **teaspoon crushed red pepper**

smoked turkey & blue cheese pasta salad

The sweet tastes of mandarin oranges, balsamic vinaigrette, and crunchy pecans are a delicious complement to the sharpness of blue cheese in this refreshingly different bow-tie pasta salad.

1½ **cups tiny bow ties or tiny shell macaroni (about 5 ounces)**

½ **cup crumbled blue cheese (2 ounces)**

⅓ **cup bottled balsamic vinaigrette or oil and vinegar salad dressing**

6 **ounces smoked turkey, cut into bite-size pieces**

1½ **cups torn curly endive and/or radicchio**

¼ **cup pecan pieces**

1 **11-ounce can mandarin orange sections, drained, or 1 avocado, seeded, peeled, and sliced**

Start to finish: 20 minutes   Makes 4 servings

Cook pasta in lightly salted water according to package directions. Drain in colander. Rinse with cold water; drain again. Transfer to a medium bowl and place in freezer to chill quickly.

Meanwhile, in a large bowl combine blue cheese and vinaigrette. Add turkey, endive, and pecans. Just before serving, add chilled pasta; toss gently to coat. Top each serving with mandarin orange sections.

Nutrition facts per serving: 333 cal., 11 g total fat (4 g sat. fat), 33 mg chol., 673 mg sodium, 43 g carbo., 1 g fiber, 17 g pro. Daily values: 7% vit. A, 22% vit. C, 8% calcium, 13% iron

cheese crumbles

Cheeses once considered exotic are now widely available, and because they are so flavorful, a little goes a long way. These tangy cheeses add loads of distinctive flavor and just a hint of decadence without a lot of fat and calories. Consider flavored fetas, any of the blue cheeses (such as Gorgonzola, Maytag blue, Stilton, or Roquefort), goat cheese (chèvre), Parmesan or Pecorino Romano, or an extra-sharp white Vermont cheddar.

chilled tortellini with lemon-ginger sauce

Keep cool in the kitchen in more ways than one with this cold pasta salad that's a breeze to put together. Lemon chicken tortellini is bejeweled with fresh fruit, then tossed with a yogurt-based lemon-ginger dressing that's as light as a feather.

Start to finish: 18 minutes   Makes 4 servings

Cook pasta according to package directions. Drain in colander. Rinse with cold water until completely cool; drain again.

Meanwhile, in a large mixing bowl stir together yogurt, ginger, and, if desired, poppy seed. Gently fold in cooled pasta and desired fruit. Serve pasta mixture on lettuce.

Nutrition facts per serving: 265 cal., 4 g total fat (2 g sat. fat), 29 mg chol., 234 mg sodium, 45 g carbo., 3 g fiber, 12 g pro. Daily values: 3% vit. A, 23% vit. C, 8% calcium, 10% iron

1 9-ounce package refrigerated lemon chicken tortellini or cheese tortellini

1 8-ounce carton lemon low-fat yogurt

½ teaspoon ground ginger

½ teaspoon poppy seed (optional)

2 cups fresh fruit (choose from raspberries, blackberries, blueberries, halved seedless grapes, sliced strawberries, and/or cubed cantaloupe or honeydew melon)

4 cups shredded lettuce

white bean
& sausage rigatoni

Reminiscent of a wonderful baked Italian casserole that comes bubbling from the oven, this dish is done on the stovetop instead, so it's ready to put on the table in less than half the time. Snipped fresh basil adds a licoricelike freshness.

8 ounces dried rigatoni pasta

1 15-ounce can white kidney (cannellini), great northern, or navy beans, rinsed and drained

1 14½-ounce can Italian-style stewed tomatoes, undrained

6 ounces cooked smoked turkey sausage, sliced ½ inch thick

⅓ cup snipped fresh basil

¼ cup shaved or finely shredded Asiago cheese (1 ounce)

Start to finish: 20 minutes   Makes 4 servings

Cook pasta according to package directions, except do not add salt to cooking water; drain. Return pasta to hot pan.

Meanwhile, in a large saucepan combine beans, undrained tomatoes, and sausage; heat through. Add bean mixture and basil to cooked pasta; toss gently to combine. Sprinkle individual servings with cheese.

Nutrition facts per serving: 401 cal., 6 g total fat (1 g sat. fat), 32 mg chol., 964 mg sodium, 67 g carbo., 5 g fiber, 25 g pro. Daily values: 8% vit. A, 19% vit. C, 12% calcium, 28% iron

shanghai pork lo mein

Forget takeout. Stir-fry this Chinese specialty in 20 minutes—far less time than it takes to place a restaurant order and pick it up. Serve it with hot jasmine or oolong tea and fortune cookies from the grocery store and you won't miss a thing!

63

Start to finish: 20 minutes   Makes 4 servings

Cook noodles according to package directions; drain. Meanwhile, in a wok or large skillet stir-fry pork in hot oil for 3 minutes, adding more oil if necessary. Add bok choy; stir fry about 2 minutes more or until pork is no longer pink and bok choy is crisp-tender.

Add the broth, orange juice, soy sauce, sesame oil, and red pepper; bring to boiling. Stir in the cooked noodles. Cook for 1 minute, stirring occasionally. Stir in orange sections.

Nutrition facts per serving: 323 cal., 7 g total fat (1 g sat. fat), 40 mg chol., 1,337 mg sodium, 45 g carbo., 1 g fiber, 20 g pro. Daily values: 5% vit. A, 30% vit. C, 3% calcium, 11% iron

6 ounces dried somen or fine egg noodles or angel hair pasta

8 ounces pork tenderloin, halved lengthwise and sliced ¼ inch thick

2 teaspoons cooking oil

2 cups sliced bok choy

¾ cup reduced-sodium chicken broth

¼ cup orange juice

3 tablespoons reduced-sodium soy sauce or regular soy sauce

2 teaspoons toasted sesame oil

¼ to ½ teaspoon crushed red pepper

1 11-ounce can mandarin orange sections, drained, or 2 large oranges, peeled and sectioned

big on
vegetables,
grains, & beans

dilled tuna & orzo

Here's pasta salad, Scandinavian style. Light and lemony, this tuna salad with tiny ricelike orzo brightened by roasted red sweet pepper and crisp cucumber is delicious served warm or chilled—so you can make it fast, and make it ahead.

Start to finish: 20 minutes   Makes 4 servings

Cook orzo according to package directions. Drain in colander. Rinse with cold water; drain again. Transfer to a large bowl. Add tuna or salmon, cucumber, and roasted sweet pepper to orzo.

For dressing, in a screw-top jar combine mustard, olive oil, lemon juice, and dill. Cover and shake well. Pour over tuna mixture; toss gently to coat. Season to taste with salt and black pepper. Serve warm or chilled.

Nutrition facts per serving: 383 cal., 11 g total fat (2 g sat. fat), 17 mg chol., 209 mg sodium, 51 g carbo., 1 g fiber, 20 g pro. Daily values: 29% vit. A, 25% vit. C, 1% calcium, 20% iron

Note: To poach fresh tuna or salmon, see "Poached to Perfection" on page 44.

1½ cups orzo (rosamarina)

6 ounces poached* or canned tuna or salmon, skinned, boned, and broken into chunks (about 1 cup)

½ cup chopped cucumber

2 tablespoons drained and snipped roasted red sweet pepper

2 tablespoons Dijon-style mustard

2 tablespoons olive oil

1 tablespoon lemon juice

2 teaspoons snipped fresh dill

polenta with fresh tomato sauce

Making polenta the traditional way takes a strong stirring hand and time for cooking, chilling, and slicing. This expeditious version serves up medallions of polenta that are crisp on the outside and creamy on the inside, atop a rosemary-olive tomato sauce.

Start to finish: 18 minutes   Makes 4 servings

For sauce, in a medium saucepan heat 2 teaspoons of the oil and the garlic over medium heat. Add tomatoes; cook for 2 minutes. Stir in olives and rosemary. Bring to boiling; reduce heat. Simmer, uncovered, for 8 minutes, stirring occasionally. Season to taste with salt and pepper.

Meanwhile, cut polenta into 8 slices. In a large nonstick skillet or on a griddle heat the remaining 2 teaspoons oil over medium heat. Add polenta; cook about 6 minutes or until golden brown, turning once. Sprinkle with cheese. Serve atop tomato sauce.

Nutrition facts per serving: 226 cal., 10 g total fat (3 g sat. fat), 16 mg chol., 608 mg sodium, 27 g carbo., 5 g fiber, 8 g pro. Daily values: 11% vit. A, 35% vit. C, 9% calcium, 4% iron

4 teaspoons olive oil

½ teaspoon bottled minced garlic

6 plum tomatoes, coarsely chopped (about 2 cups)

¼ cup pitted halved kalamata olives or sliced pitted ripe olives

2 teaspoons snipped fresh rosemary or 2 tablespoons snipped fresh thyme

1 16-ounce package prepared polenta

½ cup shredded smoked Gouda or Swiss cheese (2 ounces)

herbs for superb flavor

Fresh herbs turn ordinary dishes into extraordinary ones. Some herbs—typically those with a sturdier constitution such as rosemary, bay leaf, and sage—are good for long-simmering or roasting. More delicate fresh herbs—such as basil, coriander, dill, and oregano—are best added right at the end of cooking. To substitute dry herbs for fresh, simply use one-third the amount of fresh herb called for in a recipe. (If a recipe uses 1 tablespoon fresh herb, add 1 teaspoon dry.)

mediterranean bread salad

Good bread is a cornerstone of the Mediterranean diet. It is baked and eaten fresh every day. If there is any left over, ingenious and frugal cooks put *pappa al pommodoro* (tomato and bread soup) or *panzanella* (bread salad) on the next day's menu.

4 cups cubed sourdough bread
(about 1-inch cubes)

Nonstick olive oil spray coating

¼ teaspoon garlic salt

6 cups purchased torn mixed salad
greens

1 15-ounce can white kidney
(cannellini) beans, rinsed and
drained

1 small yellow summer squash or
zucchini, halved lengthwise
and sliced

2 plum tomatoes, coarsely chopped

½ cup bottled balsamic vinaigrette or
oil and vinegar salad dressing

½ cup finely shredded Parmesan or
Romano cheese (2 ounces)

Start to finish: 20 minutes   Makes 4 servings

Place bread cubes on a foil-lined baking sheet. Spray bread lightly with nonstick coating. Sprinkle evenly with garlic salt. Bake in a 400° oven about 10 minutes or until lightly browned.

Meanwhile, in a large bowl combine greens, beans, squash, tomatoes, and vinaigrette. Add bread cubes; toss gently to coat. Sprinkle each serving with cheese.

Nutrition facts per serving: 273 cal., 6 g total fat (0 g sat. fat), 10 mg chol., 761 mg sodium, 45 g carbo., 7 g fiber, 17 g pro. Daily values: 8% vit. A, 44% vit. C, 16% calcium, 20% iron

versatile **beans**

Beans of all kinds are great as centerpieces of vegetarian dishes not only because they're high in protein and fiber and low in fat, but because they add a heartiness and substance similar to what meat offers. From the tiniest navy bean to the broadest fava, they come in a great variety and have great versatility. Because of their almost universally mild flavor and creamy texture, you can easily substitute one kind for another. Canned beans are the ultimate in convenience, but be sure to rinse them, as their liquid is high in sodium. Dried beans tend to be more economical and offer greater variety if you can spare the soaking and cooking time.

tomatillo & black bean quesadillas

Tomatillos—small, pale green fruits covered with a thin, papery husk that's removed before they're eaten—add their crisp, green tomatolike texture and hint of lemon-apple essence to these veggie-packed quesadillas.

Start to finish: 20 minutes   Makes 4 servings

In a large nonstick skillet cook and stir tomatillos, carrot, and cumin in butter over medium-high heat for 2 to 3 minutes or until vegetables are crisp-tender. Add beans; cook and stir about 2 minutes more or until heated through. Transfer to a bowl; set aside.

In same skillet cook one tortilla over medium heat for 15 seconds. Turn over; sprinkle with ¼ cup of the cheese. Spoon one-fourth of the bean mixture over bottom half of tortilla; top with 1 tablespoon of the salsa. Fold tortilla in half, pressing gently. Cook 1 to 2 minutes more or until cheese is melted. Transfer to a baking sheet; keep warm in a 300° oven. Repeat with the remaining tortillas, cheese, and bean mixture and 3 tablespoons of the salsa. Serve warm with remaining salsa.

Nutrition facts per serving: 300 cal., 13 g total fat (7 g sat. fat), 28 mg chol., 663 mg sodium, 35 g carbo., 6 g fiber, 17 g pro. Daily values: 51% vit. A, 22% vit. C, 25% calcium, 24% iron

- ¾ **cup coarsely chopped tomatillos or coarsely shredded zucchini**
- ½ **cup coarsely shredded carrot**
- 1½ **teaspoons ground cumin**
- 1 **teaspoon butter or olive oil**
- 1 **15-ounce can black beans, rinsed and drained**
- 4 **8-inch flour tortillas**
- 1 **cup shredded Monterey Jack cheese (4 ounces)**
- ½ **cup salsa**

tomato, mozzarella, & polenta platter

Let your imagination run a little wild when it comes to tonight's salad supper. Instead of bread, try toasty polenta croutons. Use lettuce as the bowl and indulge in slices of delicate and creamy fresh mozzarella, garden tomatoes, and tangy kalamata olives.

Start to finish: 18 minutes   Makes 4 servings

Line a platter with butterhead lettuce leaves. Or, make a basket out of the head of butterhead lettuce by removing center leaves (shown at left). Arrange mozzarella, tomatoes, and basil leaves atop, leaving room for polenta.

In a large nonstick skillet, cook polenta slices in hot oil over medium heat 4 to 6 minutes or until warm and lightly browned, turning once. Add polenta and olives to platter or basket. Serve with dressing.

Nutrition facts per serving: 395 cal., 25 g total fat (9 g sat. fat), 44 mg chol., 928 mg sodium, 30 g carbo., 5 g fiber, 16 g pro. Daily values: 26% vit. A, 44% vit. C, 27% calcium, 5% iron

1 large head butterhead (Boston or Bibb) lettuce

8 ounces fresh mozzarella cheese, sliced

2 medium red tomatoes, cut into wedges

2 medium yellow tomatoes, sliced

¼ cup basil leaves

1 16-ounce package prepared polenta, cut into ¾-inch-thick slices

2 teaspoons olive oil

⅓ cup kalamata olives

¼ cup bottled red wine vinegar and oil dressing

mixed bean
& portobello ragout

Ragout is simply a thick, savory stew of French origin. This healthy, meatless ragout features a host of legumes and meaty portobellos, which are oversize brown mushrooms with an Italian-sounding name. Serve it with crusty bread.

70

- 1 10-ounce package frozen baby lima beans
- 1 cup fresh green beans, cut into 1-inch pieces
- 1½ cups sliced and halved fresh portobello mushrooms or sliced white mushrooms (about 4 ounces)
- 1 tablespoon olive oil
- 1 tablespoon cold water
- 2 teaspoons cornstarch
- 1 14½-ounce can Cajun- or Italian-style stewed tomatoes
- 1 cup canned garbanzo beans, rinsed and drained

Start to finish: 20 minutes   Makes 4 servings

Cook lima beans and green beans in lightly salted water according to lima bean package directions; drain.

Meanwhile, in a large skillet cook mushrooms in hot oil over medium heat for 5 minutes, stirring occasionally. Combine water and cornstarch; stir into mushrooms. Stir in undrained tomatoes and garbanzo beans. Cook and stir until thickened and bubbly. Cook and stir for 2 minutes more. Stir in cooked beans; heat through.

Nutrition facts per serving: 214 cal., 5 g total fat (1 g sat. fat), 0 mg chol., 528 mg sodium, 36 g carbo., 10 g fiber, 10 g pro. Daily values: 11% vit. A, 39% vit. C, 6% calcium, 25% iron

dilled spinach soup

The essence of summer in a bowl. There are few things so satisfying at the end of a warm summer day than sitting down to a refreshing cold soup seasoned with fragrant herbs. Pair it with purchased croissants and follow it with fresh peaches for dessert.

72

9 cups packaged prewashed spinach
   (about 10 ounces)

2 cups milk

1 small onion, cut up

2 tablespoons snipped fresh dill

1 teaspoon lemon-pepper seasoning

2 8-ounce cartons plain fat-free yogurt

1 cup cubed cooked chicken or ham
   or cooked small shrimp

   Edible flowers (such as nasturtiums)
   and/or toasted slivered almonds
   (optional)

Start to finish: 18 minutes   Makes 4 servings

In a blender container or food processor bowl combine about one-third of the spinach, 1 cup of the milk, the onion, dill, and lemon-pepper seasoning. Cover; blend or process until nearly smooth. Add another one-third of the spinach; cover and blend until smooth. Pour blended mixture into a serving bowl or large storage container.

In the blender container or food processor bowl combine remaining spinach, remaining milk, and the yogurt; cover and blend until nearly smooth. Stir into the mixture in serving bowl; stir in chicken. Serve immediately or cover and store in refrigerator up to 24 hours.

To serve, ladle into 4 soup bowls. If desired, garnish each serving with edible flowers and slivered almonds.

Nutrition facts per serving: 217 cal., 6 g total fat (2 g sat. fat), 45 mg chol., 508 mg sodium, 18 g carbo., 2 g fiber, 24 g pro. Daily values: 55% vit. A, 37% vit. C, 37% calcium, 17% iron

crop top pesto pizza

The "crop top" in the name of this savory pie refers to the garden of vegetables that crowns the chewy Boboli-bread crust. Start with purchased basil-rich pesto as a quick sauce, then top it with your favorite vegetables and a four-cheese blend.

74

1   **12-inch Italian bread shell (Boboli)**

¼   **cup purchased pesto with basil or dried tomato**

¼   **teaspoon ground red pepper**

1   **cup shredded pizza cheese (4 ounces)**

1   **cup torn spinach or baby spinach**

4   **roma tomatoes, sliced**

1   **small red onion, cut into very thin wedges (about ½ cup)**

8   **pitted Greek black olives, sliced***

Start to finish: 20 minutes   Makes 6 servings

Place bread shell on a 12-inch pizza pan. Skim excess oil off pesto. In a small bowl combine pesto and red pepper; spread over bread shell. Sprinkle with ¾ cup of the cheese.

Top with spinach, tomatoes, and onion. Sprinkle with remaining cheese and the olives. Bake in a 400° oven for 10 to 15 minutes or until pizza is heated through and cheese is melted.

Nutrition facts per serving: 358 cal., 17 g total fat (3 g sat. fat), 18 mg chol., 650 mg sodium, 38 g carbo., 3 g fiber, 16 g pro. Daily values: 11% vit. A, 21% vit. C, 17% calcium, 13% iron

Note: You can substitute 3 tablespoons sliced pitted ripe olives for the Greek olives if you prefer.

healthy hummus sandwiches

Apart from the kabob, no food from the Arab world is better known than hummus, a garlicky chickpea puree flavored with lemon juice and the creamy sesame butter called tahini. Traditionally, it's served with warm pita bread for dipping.

Start to finish: 15 minutes   Makes 2 servings

If desired, toast bread. Spread one side of each bread slice with hummus. Layer the alfalfa sprouts, cucumber, radishes, tomato, and cheese between the bread slices.

Nutrition facts per serving: 371 cal., 14 g total fat (5 g sat. fat), 20 mg chol., 643 mg sodium, 45 g carbo., 1 g fiber, 18 g pro. Daily values: 9% vit. A, 34% vit. C, 25% calcium, 23% iron

about **sprouts**

Alfalfa sprouts, tiny green and white shoots that sprout from alfalfa seeds, add a mildly nutty flavor and crunch to sandwiches and salads. Choose alfalfa sprouts with bright green tops and crisp shoots. Fresh sprouts are available year-round. Store them loosely covered in the refrigerator for up to four days.

- 4 slices whole grain bread or 2 hoagie buns, split
- ⅔ cup hummus
- ½ cup alfalfa sprouts
- 16 thin slices unpeeled cucumber or zucchini (about ½ cup)
- ¼ cup thinly sliced radishes (about 4 radishes)
- 1 small tomato, cut into 4 slices
- 2 ounces reduced-fat Monterey Jack cheese, sliced

inspirations
from the deli

chutney-chicken salad

Curry powder and sweet-hot mango chutney add exotic touches to classic chicken salad with red grapes. Serve it atop full-flavored salad greens with a side of fresh cherries, or try it as a sandwich filling for croissants or wraps.

Start to finish: 20 minutes   Makes 4 servings

In a shallow baking pan spread almonds in a single layer. Bake in a 350° oven for 5 to 10 minutes or until nuts are a light golden brown, stirring once or twice to prevent overbrowning. Cool slightly.

Meanwhile, in a large mixing bowl combine chutney, mayonnaise dressing, and curry powder. Add chicken, grapes, and toasted nuts; toss gently to coat. Serve on lettuce leaves.

Nutrition facts per serving: 311 cal., 16 g total fat (4 g sat. fat), 76 mg chol., 118 mg sodium, 20 g carbo., 2 g fiber, 21 g pro. Daily values: 15% vit. A, 10% vit. C, 3% calcium, 12% iron

¼ cup sliced or slivered almonds

¼ cup mango chutney, snipped

2 tablespoons light mayonnaise
    dressing or plain low-fat yogurt

1 teaspoon curry powder

2 cups shredded or chopped
    deli-roasted chicken or
    turkey breast

1 cup seedless red grapes, halved

   Lettuce leaves

roasted vegetable & pastrami panini

To Italians, panini simply means sandwiches. To American chefs, panini is a trendy title for selling the same. For a special textured effect, cook this Italian-style provolone, vegetable, and pastrami melt in a waffle iron instead of a skillet.

78

4 **thin slices provolone cheese (2 ounces)**

8 **½-inch-thick slices sourdough or Vienna bread**

1 **cup roasted or grilled vegetables from the deli or deli-marinated vegetables, coarsely chopped**

4 **thin slices pastrami (3 ounces)**

1 **tablespoon olive oil or basil-flavored olive oil**

Start to finish: 15 minutes   Makes 4 servings

Place a cheese slice on 4 of the bread slices. Spread vegetables evenly over cheese. Top with pastrami and remaining bread slices. Brush the outsides of sandwiches with oil.

Preheat a large nonstick skillet or griddle* over medium heat. Add the sandwiches; cook for 4 to 6 minutes or until sandwiches are golden brown and cheese is melted, turning once. Halve sandwiches.

Nutrition facts per serving: 254 cal., 9 g total fat (3 g sat. fat), 30 mg chol., 658 mg sodium, 30 g carbo., 1 g fiber, 13 g pro. Daily values: 46% vit. A, 38% vit. C, 13% calcium, 13% iron

Note: Or, cook sandwiches in a preheated waffle iron brushed with oil (as pictured, at right).

greek pitas

Add plum tomatoes and fresh dill to a deli-made creamy cucumber and onion salad to create hearty beef sandwiches that are pleasingly out of the ordinary.

1 cup creamy cucumber and onion
  salad from the deli*

½ cup chopped plum tomatoes

1 teaspoon snipped fresh dill

4 wheat or white pita bread rounds

12 ounces thinly sliced cooked deli
  roast beef

Start to finish: 12 minutes   Makes 4 servings

In a medium bowl combine cucumber and onion salad, tomatoes, and dill. Cut pita rounds in half crosswise. Line pita halves with roast beef and fill with salad mixture.

Nutrition facts per serving: 380 cal., 10 g total fat (3 g sat. fat), 82 mg chol., 427 mg sodium, 39 g carbo., 1 g fiber, 34 g pro. Daily values: 2% vit. A, 12% vit. C, 3% calcium, 21% iron

Note: For homemade cucumber and onion salad, combine 3 tablespoons plain low-fat yogurt, 2 teaspoons vinegar, and ½ teaspoon sugar. Add 1 small cucumber, thinly sliced (about 1 cup), and ½ of a small onion, thinly sliced (¼ cup); toss gently to coat. Season to taste with salt.

meal in a pocket

Pita bread—with its delicate flavor, tender texture, and handy mess-conserving pocket—takes the sandwich to new heights. Try these ideas for more super-quick fillings for the ingenious pita: deli chicken salad with additional celery and peppery radishes stirred in for crunch and color; Italian beef and provolone topped off with deli olive or pepper salad; deli rotisserie-roasted chicken breast and deli ham or precooked bacon tucked into a pita with mayonnaise, tomatoes, lettuce, and Swiss cheese.

ham & broccoli risotto

Traditional risotto, an Italian rice dish, requires constant stirring for about 20 minutes. It's worth the effort when you have the time. When you don't, opt for this equally tasty one-pot meal that features brown rice.

Start to finish: 20 minutes   Makes 4 servings

In a medium saucepan bring broth and water to boiling. Stir in rice. Return to boiling; reduce heat. Simmer, covered, about 10 minutes or until liquid is absorbed. Remove from heat.

Stir in broccoli, ham, milk, and dried tomatoes. Cover and let stand for 5 minutes. Sprinkle individual servings with cheese.

Nutrition facts per serving: 213 cal., 6 g total fat (1 g sat. fat), 29 mg chol., 911 mg sodium, 24 g carbo., 3 g fiber, 17 g pro. Daily values: 7% vit. A, 72% vit. C, 8% calcium, 6% iron

1   14½-ounce can reduced-sodium chicken broth

¼   cup water

1½ cups quick-cooking brown rice

1½ cups broccoli flowerets

1¼ cups cubed cooked deli ham (6 ounces)

¼   cup milk

2   tablespoons drained and snipped oil-packed dried tomatoes

¼   cup finely shredded Parmesan cheese

four
ingredients
make a meal

pesto chicken breasts
with summer squash

This study in green is all about great taste and true simplicity. Crisp-tender diamonds of zucchini accompany juicy, pan-seared chicken breasts flavored with basil-specked pesto sauce and smoky Asiago cheese (count 'em, four ingredients!).

Start to finish: 13 minutes   Makes 4 servings

Rinse chicken; pat dry. Skim 1 tablespoon oil off pesto (or substitute 1 tablespoon olive oil). In a large nonstick skillet cook chicken in hot oil over medium heat for 4 minutes.

Turn chicken; add squash. Cook for 4 to 6 minutes more or until the chicken is tender and no longer pink and squash is crisp-tender, stirring squash gently once or twice. Transfer chicken and squash to 4 dinner plates. Spread pesto over chicken; sprinkle with cheese.

Nutrition facts per serving: 169 cal., 8 g total fat (1 g sat. fat), 48 mg chol., 158 mg sodium, 4 g carbo., 1 g fiber, 19 g pro. Daily values: 2% vit. A, 4% vit. C, 4% calcium, 5% iron

4 **medium skinless, boneless chicken breast halves (about 12 ounces total)**

2 **tablespoons prepared pesto**

2 **cups finely chopped zucchini and/or yellow summer squash**

2 **tablespoons finely shredded Asiago or Parmesan cheese**

pesto possibilities

Pesto is the essence of Italy all whirled together into one heady and verdant sauce of fresh basil, olive oil, garlic, sharply flavored cheese, and rich pine nuts. Pesto is most commonly tossed with hot pasta or gnocchi (dumplings), but its uses are nearly limitless. Try spreading pesto on pizza crust instead of traditional tomato sauce before layering on the additional ingredients; top off a baked potato with pesto instead of butter or sour cream; spread it lightly over a whole chicken or under its skin before roasting; blend it with butter and serve it with grilled fish or warm bread.

chicken, pear, & blue cheese salad

The pairing of mellow pears and tangy blue cheese is naturally fresh and simple. Combine this classic twosome with packaged assorted greens and rotisserie chicken from the deli, and you've got a dinner that's naturally elegant as well.

Start to finish: 15 minutes   Makes 4 servings

In a large mixing bowl combine the salad greens, chicken, and salad dressing; toss gently to coat. Divide among 4 individual salad bowls or dinner plates. Arrange pear slices on top of salads. If desired, sprinkle with freshly ground pepper.

Nutrition facts per serving: 208 cal., 6 g total fat (2 g sat. fat), 72 mg chol., 591 mg sodium, 18 g carbo., 3 g fiber, 23 g pro. Daily values: 12% vit. A, 20% vit. C, 5% calcium, 9% iron

6 cups packaged torn mixed salad greens or mesclun (about 8 ounces)

10 to 12 ounces roasted or grilled chicken breast, sliced

¾ cup bottled reduced-calorie or regular blue cheese salad dressing

2 ripe pears, cored and sliced

chunky chicken chili

Chili connoisseurs, save your long-simmering recipes for weekends and enjoy this hearty bowl o' red when you have only minutes to spare. With just four ingredients, in no time you'll have a zesty, full-flavored chicken chili that's healthful to boot.

12 ounces skinless, boneless chicken thighs

1½ cups frozen pepper stir-fry vegetables

2 15-ounce cans chili beans with spicy chili gravy

¾ cup salsa

Start to finish: 20 minutes   Makes 4 servings

Rinse chicken; pat dry. Cut into 1-inch pieces. In a large nonstick saucepan* cook and stir chicken and frozen vegetables over medium-high heat until chicken is brown. Stir in undrained chili beans and salsa. Bring to boiling; reduce heat. Simmer, uncovered, about 7 minutes or until chicken is no longer pink.

Nutrition facts per serving: 332 cal., 7 g total fat (2 g sat. fat), 91 mg chol., 916 mg sodium, 42 g carbo., 10 g fiber, 24 g pro. Daily values: 51% vit. A, 49% vit. C, 6% calcium, 24% iron

*Note: If you do not have a large nonstick saucepan, spray an unheated large saucepan with nonstick spray coating and continue as above.

tasty chili toppers
The traditional chili toppings of sour cream, grated Monterey Jack cheese, and chopped raw onion have stood the test of time because they're good. But consider these more creative ways to crown your chili: chopped red, yellow, and orange sweet peppers; minced watercress, arugula, or cilantro; snipped fresh chives or thinly sliced green onions; crumbled corn chips; crumbled crisp-cooked bacon; corn relish or salsa; crumbled queso fresco or feta cheese (plain or jalapeño-flavored).

sweet & sour shrimp

In need of immediate gratification of the culinary kind? Purchased stir-fry sauce and prechopped vegetables make extra-quick work of this already-quick-cooking wok dish.

87

Start to finish: 12 minutes   Makes 4 servings

Thaw shrimp, if frozen. Rinse shrimp; pat dry. For sauce, combine the stir-fry sauce and pineapple-orange juice; set aside. Spray an unheated nonstick wok or large skillet with nonstick spray coating. (Add oil, if necessary, during cooking.) Preheat over medium-high heat.

Stir-fry vegetables in hot wok for 3 to 5 minutes or until crisp-tender. Remove from wok. Add shrimp; stir-fry for 2 to 3 minutes or until shrimp turn pink. Push shrimp to side of wok.

Add sauce to wok. Return vegetables. Stir vegetables and shrimp into sauce. Cook and stir about 1 minute more or until heated through.

Nutrition facts per serving: 119 cal., 1 g total fat (0 g sat. fat), 131 mg chol., 666 mg sodium,
11 g carbo., 2 g fiber, 17 g pro. Daily values: 63% vit. A, 108% vit. C, 4% calcium, 16% iron

12 ounces fresh or frozen peeled and
    deveined shrimp

⅓ cup bottled stir-fry sauce

¼ cup pineapple-orange juice

3 cups assorted fresh stir-fry
   vegetables from produce
   department

one recipe,
three great dinners
caponata

A few minutes spent making one batch of caponata (the Italian cousin of the French ratatouille) provides three days' worth of dinners filled with fresh, lively, and different flavors: open-faced sandwiches, South-of-France-style omelets, and broiled fish.

2 14½-ounce cans Italian-style stewed tomatoes, undrained

1 large eggplant, cut into ½-inch cubes (about 1¼ pounds)

2 tablespoons olive oil

1 yellow, green, or red sweet pepper, coarsely chopped

¾ cup picante sauce

½ teaspoon bottled minced garlic

2 tablespoons balsamic vinegar

Start to finish: 20 minutes   Makes about 6 cups

Cut up any large tomato pieces; set aside. In a large nonstick skillet cook half of the eggplant in 1 tablespoon hot oil over medium-high heat about 3 minutes or until golden brown, stirring occasionally. Remove from skillet. Repeat with remaining eggplant and oil. Return all of the eggplant to skillet.

Stir in undrained tomatoes, sweet pepper, picante sauce, and garlic. Bring to boiling; reduce heat. Simmer, uncovered, for 4 to 5 minutes or until slightly thickened. Stir in vinegar. Cool slightly; transfer to a storage container. Cover and store in refrigerator up to 3 days. Use Caponata in the following recipes.

caponata bruschetta

Preheat broiler. Bias-slice one 8-ounce loaf baguette-style French bread into sixteen ½-inch-thick slices. If desired, brush slices with 1 tablespoon olive oil. Place the bread slices on the unheated rack of a broiler pan. Broil 4 to 5 inches from the heat for 1 to 2 minutes or until lightly toasted. Meanwhile, cook 2 cups of the Caponata in a microwave oven on 100% power (high) about 2 minutes or on the range top until heated through, stirring occasionally. Spoon the warm Caponata on top of the bread slices. Sprinkle with ¾ cup shredded pizza cheese or mozzarella cheese (3 ounces). If desired, top with 2 tablespoons shredded fresh basil. Makes 4 servings.

Nutrition facts per serving: 270 cal., 8 g total fat (3 g sat. fat), 12 mg chol., 794 mg sodium, 39 g carbo., 1 g fiber, 11 g pro. Daily values: 10% vit. A, 41% vit. C, 16% calcium, 13% iron

provençal-style omelets

Cook 2 cups of the Caponata until heated through, stirring as needed. Cover and keep warm. Meanwhile, beat together 2 cups refrigerated egg product or 8 eggs, ½ cup milk, and ¼ teaspoon each of salt and pepper. For each omelet, in a 10-inch nonstick skillet with flared sides melt 1 tablespoon butter over medium heat; pour in half of the egg mixture. As the eggs set, lift eggs so uncooked portion flows underneath. When eggs are set but still shiny, remove from heat. Spoon half of the Caponata across center of omelet; sprinkle with 1 tablespoon grated Parmesan cheese. Fold omelet in half; cut in half and transfer to 2 dinner plates. Keep warm. Repeat to make the second omelet. Makes 4 servings.

Nutrition facts per serving: 245 cal., 14 g total fat (6 g sat. fat), 21 mg chol., 837 mg sodium, 12 g carbo., 1 g fiber, 19 g pro. Daily values: 41% vit. A, 42% vit. C, 13% calcium, 21% iron

italian halibut

Preheat broiler. Rinse four 4-ounce fresh halibut steaks cut ½ to 1 inch thick; pat dry. Brush fish with 1 tablespoon bottled Italian salad dressing. Place fish on the greased unheated rack of a broiler pan. Broil about 4 inches from the heat until fish flakes easily with a fork (allow 4 to 6 minutes per ½-inch thickness of fish). Turn 1-inch-thick steaks over halfway through broiling. Meanwhile, cook 2 cups of the Caponata in a microwave oven on 100% power (high) about 2 minutes or on the range top until heated through, stirring as needed. Spoon the Caponata over fish. Makes 4 servings.

Nutrition facts per serving: 200 cal., 7 g total fat (1 g sat. fat), 36 mg chol., 441 mg sodium, 10 g carbo., 1 g fiber, 25 g pro. Daily values: 11% vit. A, 41% vit. C, 5% calcium, 10% iron

marinated vegetables

Cool and crisp—one recipe of these tangy marinated vegetables offers three favorite fast repasts: a main-dish salad, a quick pasta dinner, and vegetarian sandwiches. Choose a mix of your favorite precut vegetables from the salad bar or produce aisle.

6 cups cut-up assorted fresh vegetables from salad bar or produce department

1 cup pitted kalamata olives or ripe olives

1 cup bottled reduced-calorie Italian salad dressing

Start to finish: 10 minutes   Makes about 7 cups

In a large bowl combine the vegetables, olives, and salad dressing; toss gently to coat. Cover and store in refrigerator up to 3 days. Use the Marinated Vegetables in the following recipes.

beyond broccoli

Broccoli and other traditional vegetables such as carrots, cauliflower, peas, and zucchini are all delicious in this recipe, but variety is the spice of life, right? Most produce departments feature a broad and tantalizing array of interesting vegetables from which to choose. Consider adding these to your mix: lightly steamed haricots verts (French for green string beans) or Italian green, purple, or yellow wax beans; sugar snap peas; julienned jicama; chopped fennel; lightly steamed asparagus; quartered baby pattypan squash; crimini mushrooms; cubed orange, red, or yellow sweet peppers; or halved pear-shaped baby tomatoes. The acid from the vinegar in the salad dressing will turn bright green vegetables a shade of olive. If that's bothersome, simply add green vegetables to the mix right before you use it.

italian marinated salad

In a medium bowl combine 2 cups of the Marinated Vegetables and 1 cup sliced cooked turkey cut into ½-inch strips or one 6½-ounce can chunk white tuna (water pack), drained and broken into chunks. Divide 5 cups packaged torn mixed salad greens among 4 dinner plates. Arrange the vegetable mixture on top of the greens. If desired, top with ¼ cup cubed smoked cheddar cheese (1 ounce). Makes 4 servings.

Nutrition facts per serving: 107 cal., 4 g total fat (1 g sat. fat), 31 mg chol., 236 mg sodium, 6 g carbo., 2 g fiber, 13 g pro. Daily values: 50% vit. A, 44% vit. C, 3% calcium, 8% iron

stir-fry shrimp & pasta

Rinse 12 ounces fresh peeled and deveined shrimp; pat dry. Cook one 9-ounce package refrigerated red sweet pepper fettuccine according to package directions. Drain; keep warm. Meanwhile, spray an unheated large nonstick skillet with nonstick spray coating. Stir-fry 2 cups of the Marinated Vegetables in the hot skillet over medium-high heat for 3 to 4 minutes or until crisp-tender. Remove vegetables. Add shrimp; stir-fry for 2 to 3 minutes or until shrimp turn pink. Return vegetables; cook and stir until heated through. Serve over pasta. Sprinkle with ½ cup crumbled goat (chèvre) or feta cheese and 2 tablespoons snipped fresh basil. Makes 4 servings.

Nutrition facts per serving: 345 cal., 10 g total fat (3 g sat. fat), 144 mg chol., 571 mg sodium, 40 g carbo., 3 g fiber, 25 g pro. Daily values: 60% vit. A, 43% vit. C, 8% calcium, 26% iron

vegetarian sandwiches

Place 3 cups of the Marinated Vegetables in a food processor bowl; cover and process until vegetables are coarsely chopped. (Or, use a sharp knife to coarsely chop the vegetables.) Spread each of 8 slices whole grain or dark rye bread with about 1½ teaspoons soft-style cream cheese with chives and onion. Spoon about ½ cup of the chopped vegetables between each pair of bread slices. If desired, top chopped vegetables with a few fresh basil or spinach leaves. Makes 4 servings.

Nutrition facts per serving: 265 cal., 13 g total fat (4 g sat. fat), 17 mg chol., 666 mg sodium, 33 g carbo., 2 g fiber, 8 g pro. Daily values: 75% vit. A, 60% vit. C, 7% calcium, 16% iron

91

mexican beans & rice

Great on its own, this savory bean and rice combo is versatile, too. Try it embellished with leaf lettuce and sliced tomatoes, topped with Cajun-style chicken breasts, or tucked into pita pockets with lean ground turkey and light sour cream.

3 cups cold cooked rice from deli or Oriental restaurant

2 15-ounce cans black, pinto, or red kidney beans, rinsed and drained

1 10-ounce package frozen peas, thawed

1 cup sliced celery

1 small red onion, chopped (½ cup)

2 4½-ounce cans diced green chili peppers, drained

⅔ cup bottled reduced-calorie Italian salad dressing

2 tablespoons lime juice

½ teaspoon ground cumin

Start to finish: 15 minutes   Makes about 9 cups (¾ cup dressing)

In a large bowl combine cooked rice, beans, peas, celery, onion, and chili peppers. Cover bowl or transfer mixture to a covered storage container. In a screw-top jar combine salad dressing, lime juice, and cumin. Cover and shake well.

Store the bean mixture and dressing separately in refrigerator up to 1 week. Use the Mexican Beans & Rice and the dressing in the following recipes.

mexican beans & rice salad

Line 4 dinner plates with leaf lettuce. Slice 2 tomatoes; arrange on top of the leaf lettuce. In a medium bowl combine 3 cups of the Mexican Beans & Rice and ¼ cup of the dressing; toss gently to coat. Spoon the mixture on top of the tomato slices. Makes 4 servings.

Nutrition facts per serving: 145 cal., 2 g total fat
(0 g sat. fat), 1 mg chol., 365 mg sodium,
28 g carbo., 5 g fiber, 8 g pro. Daily values:
4% vit. A, 27% vit. C, 5% calcium, 13% iron

blackened chicken sauté

Rinse 4 large skinless, boneless chicken breast halves (about 1 pound total); pat dry. Place each piece between 2 pieces of plastic wrap. Pound to ½-inch thickness; remove wrap. Sprinkle the chicken with 1 tablespoon blackened steak seasoning or Cajun seasoning. In a large nonstick skillet cook chicken in 1 tablespoon hot olive oil over medium-high heat for 4 minutes, turning once. Reduce heat to medium. Cook, covered, for 4 to 6 minutes more or until chicken is no longer pink. Meanwhile, combine 3 cups of the Mexican Beans & Rice, ¼ cup of the dressing, and ¼ cup shredded carrot; toss. Serve chicken atop bean mixture. Makes 4 servings.

Nutrition facts per serving: 296 cal., 9 g total fat
(2 g sat. fat), 60 mg chol., 555 mg sodium,
28 g carbo., 5 g fiber, 29 g pro. Daily values:
27% vit. A, 18% vit. C, 7% calcium, 20% iron

turkey salad pitas

In a large nonstick skillet cook 8 ounces lean ground raw turkey until turkey is no longer pink. Drain well. Stir in 3 cups of the Mexican Beans & Rice and ¼ cup of the dressing. Cut 3 white or wheat pita bread rounds in half crosswise. Spread the insides of the pita halves with ¼ cup light dairy sour cream. Fill with the turkey and Mexican bean mixture. Sprinkle with 2 tablespoons snipped cilantro, if desired. Makes 6 servings.

Nutrition facts per serving: 350 cal., 8 g total fat
(2 g sat. fat), 24 mg chol., 645 mg sodium,
53 g carbo., 4 g fiber, 20 g pro. Daily values:
3% vit. A, 16% vit. C, 10% calcium, 23% iron

By making a few conversions, cooks in Australia, Canada, and the United Kingdom can use the recipes in Better Homes and Gardens® *Fresh and Simple*™ *20-Minute Super Suppers* with confidence. The charts on this page provide a guide for converting measurements from the U.S. customary system, which is used throughout this book, to the imperial and metric systems. There also is a conversion table for oven temperatures to accommodate the differences in oven calibrations.

Product Differences: Most of the ingredients called for in the recipes in this book are available in English-speaking countries. However, some are known by different names. Here are some common American ingredients and their possible counterparts:

- Sugar is granulated or castor sugar.
- Powdered sugar is icing sugar.
- All-purpose flour is plain household flour or white flour. When self-rising flour is used in place of all-purpose flour in a recipe that calls for leavening, omit the leavening agent (baking soda or baking powder) and salt.
- Light corn syrup is golden syrup.
- Cornstarch is cornflour.
- Baking soda is bicarbonate of soda.
- Vanilla is vanilla essence.
- Green, red, or yellow sweet peppers are capsicums.
- Golden raisins are sultanas.

Volume and Weight: Americans traditionally use cup measures for liquid and solid ingredients. The chart, above right, shows the approximate imperial and metric equivalents. If you are accustomed to weighing solid ingredients, the following approximate equivalents will be helpful.

- 1 cup butter, castor sugar, or rice = 8 ounces = about 250 grams
- 1 cup flour = 4 ounces = about 125 grams
- 1 cup icing sugar = 5 ounces = about 150 grams

Spoon measures are used for smaller amounts of ingredients. Although the size of the tablespoon varies slightly in different countries, for practical purposes and for recipes in this book, a straight substitution is all that's necessary.

Measurements made using cups or spoons always should be level unless stated otherwise.

Equivalents: U.S. = Australia/U.K.

⅛ teaspoon = 0.5 ml
¼ teaspoon = 1 ml
½ teaspoon = 2 ml
1 teaspoon = 5 ml
1 tablespoon = 1 tablespoon
¼ cup = 2 tablespoons = 2 fluid ounces = 60 ml
⅓ cup = ¼ cup = 3 fluid ounces = 90 ml
½ cup = ⅓ cup = 4 fluid ounces = 120 ml
⅔ cup = ½ cup = 5 fluid ounces = 150 ml
¾ cup = ⅔ cup = 6 fluid ounces = 180 ml
1 cup = ¾ cup = 8 fluid ounces = 240 ml
1¼ cups = 1 cup
2 cups = 1 pint
1 quart = 1 liter
½ inch = 1.27 cm
1 inch = 2.54 cm

Baking Pan Sizes

American	Metric
8×1½-inch round baking pan	20×4-cm cake tin
9×1½-inch round baking pan	23×3.5-cm cake tin
11×7×1½-inch baking pan	28×18×4-cm baking tin
13×9×2-inch baking pan	30×20×3-cm baking tin
2-quart rectangular baking dish	30×20×3-cm baking tin
15×10×1-inch baking pan	30×25×2-cm baking tin (Swiss roll tin)
9-inch pie plate	22×4- or 23×4-cm pie plate
7- or 8-inch springform pan	18- or 20-cm springform or loose-bottom cake tin
9×5×3-inch loaf pan	23×13×7-cm or 2-pound narrow loaf tin or pâté tin
1½-quart casserole	1.5-liter casserole
2-quart casserole	2-liter casserole

Oven Temperature Equivalents

Fahrenheit Setting	Celsius Setting*	Gas Setting
300°F	150°C	Gas Mark 2 (slow)
325°F	160°C	Gas Mark 3 (moderately slow)
350°F	180°C	Gas Mark 4 (moderate)
375°F	190°C	Gas Mark 5 (moderately hot)
400°F	200°C	Gas Mark 6 (hot)
425°F	220°C	Gas Mark 7
450°F	230°C	Gas Mark 8 (very hot)
Broil		Grill

* *Electric and gas ovens may be calibrated using Celsius. However, for an electric oven, increase the Celsius setting 10 to 20 degrees when cooking above 160°C. For convection or forced-air ovens (gas or electric), lower the temperature setting 10°C when cooking at all heat levels.*